Flying Model Airplanes & Helicopters By Radio Control

No. 825
$7.95

Flying Model Airplanes & Helicopters By Radio Control

By Edward L. Safford

TAB BOOKS
Blue Ridge Summit, Pa. 17214

Preface

It has been several years since I have been active in one of my favorite hobbies: building and flying radio-controlled model airplanes. It has always provided rewards, fascination, and satisfaction as nothing else ever could. Realizing that a good many years had elapsed, I began a series of studies to see what had happened in this field since the days when I used to make my own escapements and servos, feeling lucky if I got my planes up and down all in one piece. Today this hobby presents a scene of tiny (and some not so tiny) model airplanes whirling, looping, diving, and edge-flying through every maneuver imaginable without a bit of hesitation, without any strings or wires—nothing connecting them with the ground—and each under the perfect (radio) control of every representative of humanity.

I knew that during my inactivity, technology, being what it is, was growing at an exponential rate. Surely, I felt, some almost unbelievable developments must have taken place. My feelings were verified.

Yes, the hobby has changed—*advanced* is a better word; it has expanded in concept and in the number of its participants. That is what this book is all about: to tell you about the hobby today and the people in it.

To get meaningful information, I personally contacted as many modelers as possible in the United States. This survey received responses from young and old of both sexes in every walk of life; I asked about what they flew and how they flew it, and how they felt about this wonderful sport. The sample was large and random enough to allow me to say, with little reservation, it is representative of the majority of RC (radio-controlled) model enthusiasts in the United States; much of the advice given throughout this book comes directly from these willing and helpful respondents.

My survey was conducted by mailing questionnaires; I am happy to say that 85% of those were completed and returned. This was followed up by personal letters, telephone conversations, and visits. Much of the data from manufacturers was obtained by personal correspondence, phone calls, and visiting plants that make RC equipment. It was also my pleasure, during this investigation, to have been invited to many club meetings where, at both clubhouses and flying fields, I met some of the finest people you could ever want to associate with. All were very helpful in assisting me in my quest for information.

In general I found that the RC airplane modeler is a reasonably intelligent, well adjusted individual making his own contribution to society through his occupation; he is enmeshed in his hobby, has made a considerable investment in effort, and is a gregarious sort who joins others for the fun of a common interest at social events, both at and away from the model-flying field. He takes pride in the technical knowledge he has of his hobby, and is not afraid to experiment. (The results of some of these experiments have been included herein.)

The results of my survey, as well as some of my own ideas and concepts of how things work, how to get started, and how to develop a plan, make up the basis for this work. You won't find advice on building a multitude of different airplanes here because, according to my survey, I found that a few models (in a progressive sense) represent what is being flown by the respondents. The most basic model is discussed in greatest detail for those of you new to this hobby. There are plans for the experienced and some ideas that are possibly new to everyone. Because so many current model magazines regularly offer constructional details for model airplanes, too much of the same here presents the risk of tautology.

The electronic equipment used needs a little more treatment, because most people—indeed, even some veterans in this field—do not really understand how this part of an RC system works. There are two choices for the newcomer: buy a ready-built system or build a system from a reputable kit manufacturer. Radio amateurs will, most probably, want to go the kit route. To them I say welcome aboard and 73 from W5FKZ.

I found kit-building challenging, and rewarding in success. I feel the days of building from scratch are over. For an adequate return on money invested, in terms of getting matched parts and a proved system, building a kit is the best way to go.

To all of you who have enjoyed my previous books, and to those who have been so generous and kind in your acceptance and comments, thank you for your perusal and, I hope, acceptance of this work. To those I haven't yet met through the pages of something written, please accept my thanks for being interested in this book and using it as our first meeting ground. Happy RC flying!

E. L. Safford, Jr.

Contents

Introduction

The hobby of RC model flight is no longer the pursuit of just a few "nuts" who play with toys (as they were described a few years ago). The hobby is now enjoyed by over a hundred thousand enthusiasts—a figure obtained by extrapolating club membership information throughout the United States. Of course, I have had some club members tell me that the "nuts" must still be out there, those who continue year after year in spite of crashes, glitches, and costly pilot errors. The models are not toys but are really midget airplanes requiring scientific and engineering skills to make and fly them. Yet anyone can learn the necessary skills and participate regardless of his background.

The statistic I cited may only represent a portion of those involved in this hobby indirectly; many could not be counted because they are not affiliated with dealers, manufacturers, or clubs.

The survey mentioned earlier (Preface) covered many topics through numerous questions. Of the many responses received some were delightful. One respondent wrote, "I have been building model airplanes for 25 years. I dropped the hobby for a while about ten years ago. But now, with my son, I am back in it stronger than ever." What a wonderful situation! The father/son team concept is a working reality. They are working together, enjoying something in which they both can participate and find companionship (which, in so many parent-child relationships, is rare nowadays). Mom, of course, can be a part of this hobby too; a mother or daughter often completely outfly the menfolk.

AREAS OF INTEREST

The hobby is not just mechanical in interest, it is also social. Flying events at flying fields are family affairs. Club meetings are arranged so that members' accomplishments, new ideas, and progress can be discussed, and newcomers can be taught. While snacking on coffee and sandwiches, members can listen to talks by highly qualified guests. Dances are held, parties given, doorprizes awarded—fun for everyone.

Then there are the contests, local fly-ins where one club invites others to come and join them for a flying session with, perhaps, prizes for best pattern maneuver, best aerobatic demonstration, best model, most ingenious technical development, most complex control system, and so forth. Fly-ins are being held almost daily across the United States.

The number of clubs registered with the AMA (Academy of Model Aeronautics, 806 Fifteenth St. NW., Washington D. C.) is 1014; all are engaged in many aspects of radio-controlled flight.

The average club membership is 58, although not all of these are always active. It is my estimation that there are some 58,800 persons in the United States who are members of clubs affiliated with the AMA.

Now consider those rugged individualists who choose not to be a member of a club, those who like to go it alone yet find companionship at flying fields or other recognized flying sites, or who only occasionally enter contests. They represent, as indicated by my survey, 19.7% of all model flyers, or about 11,585. That would bring the total of active model-airplane enthusiasts to 70,400, a figure slightly lower than that estimated by the AMA (which sets the figure at 75,000). In considering the hobbyists in this field we cannot neglect the radio amateur who is primarily interested in the electronics aspects of the hobby as supplementary to his main interest.

It has been estimated that of the 1½ million radio amateurs who pursue their hobby (in the United States), approximately 8% are interested in the RC facet of electronics and communications. This could swell the total by another 80,000 who are less devoted but participate in the hobby

11

directly or indirectly at some time. So we are now considering some 150,000 persons interested enough in the hobby to be actively engaged in it (not to mention those concerned with the hobby because of associated jobs, manufacturing, selling, or publishing). A graph has been provided as Appendix A to illustrate the geographical distribution of RC aircraft clubs. Notice that (without surprise) California leads the way with the largest number of clubs, while Vermont and Utah tie for last place with one club each. It wouldn't be unreasonable to assume that since California and Oregon have long been centers of the aircraft industry, persons who love their work in this field would join a club and pursue this hobby. Appendix B shows the distribution of types of model aircraft activity.

Why do people take up radio-controlled model airplane flying? I asked the persons I contacted to rate five areas of the hobby, asking which gave them the most pleasure and which the least, using a scale of 1 to 5; 1 represented the greatest pleasure and 5, the least.

The responses showed, beyond question, that *flying* RC airplanes gave the greatest pleasure with *building* running second; flying and building together accounted for 95.3% of the vote for most pleasurable. Most said that club activities were somewhat pleasurable, their rating running in the middle of the scale; I believe this indicates a need for a second look at what club meetings consist of, to find out how to make them more pleasurable. (Often it is the time or distance involved in attending meetings and conflicts with other activities that discourage more active club participation; this aspect was rated third in the survey data.)

Building and adjusting electronic equipment, yet another category, ran a close race for last place with contest participation; both were rated almost equally *least pleasurable*, the former losing by a nose. Now this information is significant because electronics comprises a major part of the hobby (equipment). Because most people enjoy what they do best, I can only assume that the majority of persons who vetoed electronics as pleasurable were merely admitting to a lack of knowledge in this area. Soldering, resistors, capacitors—these are things the average citizen knows nothing about. Also, much of the RC equipment today is offered ready to fly; little if anything is required to adjust it (although batteries must be kept charged). Then, too, the equipment is complex, requiring specialized knowledge and test equipment for its repair. Adding these factors together produces good reason for the low interest. (Radio amateurs and qualified electronics technicians, of course, were most interested in this aspect.)

One reason formal contests were rated low was given by one of my contacts who said that they entailed "...too much hassle and pressure." In fairness, however, I must report that another respondent said, "[I] have participated in three fun flys—very enjoyable."

SOURCES OF INFORMATION

Through first hand visits, my survey included questions directed to various hobby dealers and shops; the answers were not always as anticipated. Thinking that I would find active, enthusiastic modelers in these shops who would be delighted to help locate model flyers, builders, or club members, I found instead young part-time salespersons who did not have a model and, for that matter, weren't even interested in having one. Need I say they had little real knowledge of model-building, mechanics, or RC procedures. When asked about specific models on display or what kind of performance one could expect from a particular kit, their answers ranged from "I don't know" to "Maybe I can get someone who can give you some answers."

The point of this is that, contrary to popular belief, the hobby dealer is *not* the first source to go to for answers to questions about the sport. Rather, the most reliable source for such information is the hobbyist himself, that is, persons in your area active in the sport. Of course, most hobby shops can direct you to patrons in the neighborhood who might be willing to assist you.

Many of the respondents to my survey declared their interest in this hobby, having known about it from reading various publications, but because they were in isolated areas, didn't know what to do or who to contact for information. For those who fit into this category, I suggest a letter to the AMA. They will help you with your special problems and, possibly, will refer you to others in your area who are hobbyists (and provide their addresses and telephone numbers).

If your specific problem needs relatively quick attention, model magazines are good sources to contact through their letters-from-readers department; responses will be published or mailed to you.

Finally, manufacturers are good sources. I have found that large, reputable firms *do* respond to inquiries and requests for information. They have, perhaps, the best, most experienced modelers in their employ.

1

Looking Back

Progress in the radio control of model aircraft has been as great as the progress in the advanced sciences. Radio control of model aircraft began slowly at just about the same time the current rocket program began. That beginning, like others, showed us that we had to crawl before we could walk, that we had to learn the refinements of balance and power before we could run.

In 1936 a magazine, *Model Aviation*, announced, "A new contest has been arranged for radio-controlled models." In the issue that followed a month later, it was reported that the radio-controlled model event had failed. "But," the publisher consoled, "we hope to see those radio-controlled models next year." No one had appeared for the first event. The following year, however, the event was successful. Six model aircraft were entered in the national model competition.

RC PIONEERS

The first to succeed in flying an RC (radio-controlled) model plane was Chester Lanzo of Cleveland. His model, hand-launched, flew directly into a nearby parking lot, where it crashed. But judges present noticed that along the way whenever Lanzo activated a control, the ship wobbled. Radio control of model aircraft had been born.

Subsequent years saw rapid progress. In 1938, a radio-controlled model took off from the ground for the first

Fig. 1-1. One tube (an RK-61), a relay, and a tuning coil make up the essentials of this early carrier-operated receiver.

time. It went up and down—just like that. Then came the biggie. In 1939 brothers Walt and Bill Goode, amateur radio operators with degrees in physics, successfully flew, by radio control, a rectangular course and a figure-8, then landed their model at their feet. Radio control of models was here to stay.

EARLY GEAR

Back in the early days, radio-controlled equipment was heavy and bulky. A gas-filled thyratron (vacuum tube), an RK-61 (Fig. 1-1), was often used. The receiver shown has a simple circuit that activates an escapement, something like the device in watches that makes the gears turn in one direction, a step at a time. The escapement allowed electrical signals to move a rudder left or right with a single rotation of its little crank (Fig. 1-2).

The single-tube receiver left much to be desired. It was adjusted so that when the transmitter's signal, *carrier*, was received, a change in current through the tube operated a relay, which operated the escapement. Receivers were tuned for maximum range by turning a tuning slug in a coil while watching a meter for maximum signal. Nowadays transmitters and receivers are matched in frequency through the use of piezoelectric crystals that are carefully calibrated at the factory.

The escapement-operated rudder always moved "bang-bang," that is, to full deflection one way or the other. In the absence of a signal, the rudder remained neutral. A pulse code was used: depressing and holding and SEND button gave *left rudder;* releasing and depressing it again commanded *right rudder*. This sequence could be reversed, and often was during a model's flight. Whenever the button was released, the rudder returned to neutral. (Most of the time one couldn't be sure what the next depress-and-hold sequence would produce.

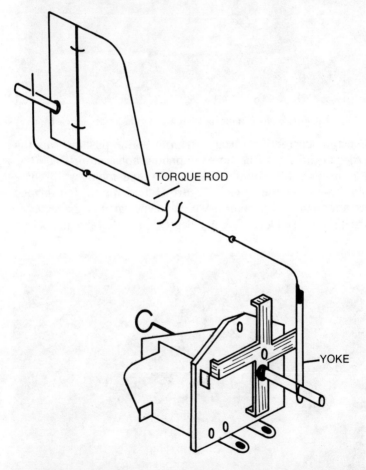

Fig. 1-2. The escapement was the basic unit that converted signals into mechanical motion. Note that the yoke is positioned to operate the rudder in the energized positions; self-neutralization occurs in the absence of a signal.

Fig. 1-3. Interior view of fuselage showing four-armed escapement.

Constant correction through frantic button pushing was the order of the day.) The series of photographs comprising Figs. 1-3 through 1-6 might bring a nostalgic memory to some old-timers in this field. Figure 1-3 shows a four-armed escapement, to the rear of which a servo arm is connected to the plane's rudder; Fig. 1-4 depicts the McNabb motorized

Fig. 1-4. McNabb motorized escapement.

Fig. 1-5. Servo arm connected to throttle valve.

escapement used for motor control; Fig. 1-5, a servo arm used to operate a throttle valve; Fig. 1-6, a *trim tab* used to correct aircraft attitude. These systems are different from current methods of adjusting trim by moving a lever on the transmitter.

Much of the homemade equipment used in the early days of the hobby was taken from amateur radio. The frequencies

Fig. 1-6. Trim tab (encircled).

Fig. 1-7. The transmitter in this photo (upper left) is mounted on the antenna pole to reduce signal losses; the power supply rests atop a car bumper plate, and the handheld control box is at the end of a long cable. The aircraft, a modified Rudderbug, contains a receiver using an RK-61 tube.

used were within the 6-meter radio band. Power was obtained from automobile batteries and converters; this arrangement provided 6 volts for tube filaments and 350 to 400 volts for tube plates. Power output was between 5 and 10 watts. One primitive system used by W6JRG in San Diego is shown in Fig. 1-7.

Not only were early receivers sensitive to any kind of electrical disturbance, they were also sensitive to anything near their antennas. One never knew, when launching an aircraft with this equipment in it, when a dive would occur. In an earlier book I gave a complete description of this kind of receiver and how to test and adjust it, and discussed the use of tones and various means of encoding and decoding signals. Figure 1-8 shows an early two-channel tone-operated receiver.

The battery pack required for these models was heavy, often weighing as much as 1½ pounds, and consisted of two D cells (for vacuum-tube filaments) and a 67½-volt battery (for B+). The larger battery also powered the same kind of relay/escapement shown in Fig. 1-8. Heavy? You said it! Early RC installations (Fig. 1-9) weighed up to 2 pounds, and provided only rudder and motor control. (Motor control was often accomplished through a linkage that dropped a piece of sponge rubber into the carburetor's venturi, thus causing the fuel/air mixture to richen.)

The transmitters also used *vibrator* power supplies. Using the 6- or 12-volt output of a car battery, they consisted of a vibrating switch that pulsed the battery voltage so it could be transformed to a higher value and be rectified and smoothed to provide the desired 350- to 400-volt output. In this manner a low-voltage, high-current source was used for a high-voltage, low-current output (the product of current and voltage

Fig. 1-8. The two relays shown in this receiver weigh 4 ounces apiece. They operate two escapements: one for the rudder and one for motor control.

21

Fig. 1-9. In this RC installation, the receiver is suspended on rubber bands.

remains the same). A good example of these transmitters is shown in Fig. 1-10.

Later developments in RC equipment brought the McNabb transmitter with its folded-dipole/reflector antenna, which was mounted right on the transmitter case (Fig. 1-11).

Fig. 1-10. Early homebrew radio-control transmitter.

The high operating frequency of this unit, 465 MHz, evidenced real advancement. There was a light to indicate its transmissions and a pushbutton switch that sent signals to an escapement.

The McNabb receiver used a single tube that worked like the RK-61 but was a "hard tube," unlike the thyratron. Its antenna was vastly different: a square of metal mounted under the receiver baseboard (and resonant at the operating frequency). This system proved the practicability of using very high-frequency radio control but used the transmitter's carrier only (unregulated radiation); the single-tube operation was not very reliable, however.

Fig. 1-11. Best results with the McNabb transmitter were obtained by pointing it directly at the model.

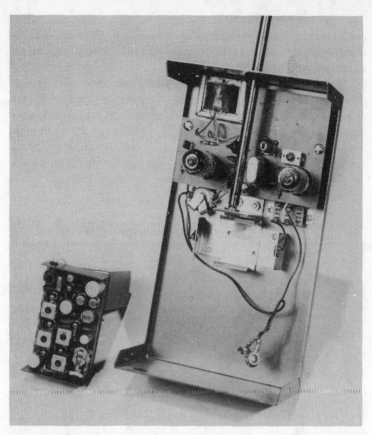

Fig. 1-12. The Venus tone-operated receiver and transmitter, although single-channel equipment, was very reliable, even when citizen's band interference was bad.

A receiver/transmitter combination that enjoyed success on the 27 MHz band, one finally allocated for RC use, was the Venus system (Fig. 1-12).

This forerunner of current equipment included a crystal-controlled transmitter and a crystal-controlled superheterodyne receiver. The single-channel tone-operated duo provided excellent reliability, unless swamped by interference from other citizen's band transmitters, or from other sources. The now-dated decoders for tones ranged from *lumped-constant* units, which were made from inductors and capacitors tuned for audio frequencies, such as 300, 650, or 950 Hz (Hertz—formerly *cycles per second*), to reed-type decoders (Fig. 1-9), which were very selective and operated on frequencies of 350, 400, 450, and 500 Hz. In a reed decoder, a reed vibrates according to a tone received, and swings over a wider arc until it touches a contact point on every swing. The current caused to flow is smoothed out by a large capacitor and operates a sensitive relay, which remains closed as long as the reed vibrates. The relay was used to operate escapements, servos, and so forth. The spark that resulted from intermittent contact was reduced by a resistance/capacitance filter placed across the reed points.

Although very selective and having multichannel capability, these decoders experienced a few problems. Often the reeds wouldn't vibrate far enough to make contact; dirt would get into the contacts; slight deviations in tone would prevent operation. But, with care and attention, many good flights were made by many with this kind of equipment. Control boxes usually incorporated external switches, "sticks," or cranks positioned so they could actuate Microswitches within.

FLIGHT PREPARATIONS

Range testing was always an important part of readying a new model for consistent performance; the practice is just as important today. I can recall walking across the sand hills of El Paso with receiver in hand and earphones in place, listening to pulsed tone signals and watching a relay to be sure it would close upon receipt of each tone pulse. (The farther away I could get without disrupting the relay's operation, the better the RC system.) At home an automatic keyer operated the transmitter. If the equipment operated within what I considered an optimum distance, I was assured I'd never lose an airplane in flight. People would stop to watch me test; some would even follow me, not knowing what I was up to, thinking, perhaps, that I had invented an electronic method of divining gold buried in the dunes.

Another vital consideration was the effects of vibration. Vibration testing consisted of activating the model's motor and holding onto the assembly for a range test. Vibration that could detract from performance was evidenced by erratic control-surface movements as the distance between transmitter and receiver increased. A second party had to operate the transmitter in accord with hand signals waved at him by the person holding the model. Various kinds of motor mounts and rubber insulators were used to support the motors. One arrangement was a rubber block with two bolts going through each end. One end of the rubber block was bolted to the motor mounts; the other had bolts that fit into the motor-mount holes. Once fastened in place, the motor was isolated from the airframe, much like the way automobile engines are from their frames. This method had disadvantages. Because the motors were flexibly mounted, they could change in alignment after a bad landing. It was also necessary to be careful that a motor didn't become disengaged from its mounting lugs or tear them out of the rubber. I liked the wooden motor mounts best. They seemed to be strong while affording adequate resilience, and they could be firmly anchored to firewalls within model planes. Today's metal motor mounts are strong, straightforward in design, and seem to overcome many of the problems experienced in earlier years (although vibration is still one of the enemies of radio-controlled models.)

Today, unlike the days when one had to go it alone, you can be taught to fly by an expert who will watch and help and who will, probably, fly your airplane to ascertain its airworthiness. Considering the cost of models and auxiliary equipment, it would be advisable to get expert help the first time out as insurance against disappointment in losing what could be a sizable investment.

Our motto in years past was, "If it will take off from the ground, it will fly; if it won't, it can't be damaged much." We approached first flights with those words in mind. If a first flight was at all manageable, that gave enough certainty that necessary adjustments to wing or motor would guarantee the second flight to be the beginning of a long and happy relationship with our planes.

Sometimes model airplanes were glide tested: running with them, with full loads but without propeller, and shoving them forward at a slight angle toward a point some 50 feet ahead on the ground. They were supposed to glide to a landing at, behind, or ahead of that spot; climbs or turns did not count in this test. If the airplane turned sharply, it didn't suffer great damage, because it was not being powered. Through trimming and other adjustments the required straight glide was eventually attained. Powering the plane's propeller could cause trouble, but if you had some control, no serious accidents occurred. The models were always statically balanced laterally and longitudinally. Adding a little weight to a wingtip to compensate for a lack of balance was commonplace. If this wasn't done before flight testing, flight problems were compounded.

There is much to learn from the past. Many modern concepts grew from past experience and experimentation. What has been learned has made model planes more reliable—even though today's RC craft carry more elaborate and sophisticated electronic systems.

Experimentation in this field has produced RC aircraft applications much less "frivolous" than spare-time fun. The military has been using *drones* (pilotless planes) since the 1940s as aerial targets for 90 and 180 millimeter guns, and later as rocket targets for guided missiles.

The first RC Army target airplanes, *OQ targets*, had triangular bodies consisting of a metal frame lightly covered with fabric; they had strong wings and tails. Controls operated a rudder, elevator, and a parachute to insure a landing in case the plane ran out of gas (if it wasn't hit first). Rather than taxiing for a takeoff, the target planes were catapulted into the air with a launching device that operated like a slingshot: it used gigantic "rubber bands." Later the launcher took the form of a dolly with wheels, tethered to a post in the center of a circular track. The airplane, secured to the dolly, provided the power for the launcher; when it went fast enough, the plane was released.

The uses of remotely controlled military aircraft of every size and description are great. For example, they are used for battlefield surveillance, bearing TV cameras as they fly low and fast over fortifications, installations, troop bivouacs, and supply depots, and sending living pictures back to HQ—using advanced techniques, and even at night.

Recently a national television network devoted air time to the possibility of using RC models as law enforcement tools in a program featuring two radio-controlled models. The police chief of Tampa and his assistants, manning the radio-controlled aircraft, demonstrated how these small planes could be used by local precincts: to attack snipers concealed in high buildings. It was clear that it would be possible to use two RC models, a decoy maneuvering furiously in front of the sniper, a second carrying a tear gas grenade, to fly directly into the sniper's area to disable him. Among the beautiful flights demonstrated to millions of viewers was a precision bomb drop, a maneuver lasting a minute or more while dense smoke streamed from an aircraft carrying a payload of 2 pounds. The aircraft were high-wing, polydihedral types with Blue Head engines; the transmitter had two control sticks. The pilot, an 18-year veteran of model flight, did a marvelous job of clearing the audience during a takeoff in a high wind. To millions it was shown that these models weren't mere toys after all.

2

Aerodynamics and the Ideal Airplanes

One thinks, as his model airplane darts swiftly through the sky, responding to his lightest touch on the controls, his smallest command, that is it alive. Glue, balsa, bolts and screws, harness wire, covering material and paint—all are brought together with time, effort, frustration, patience, and perseverance in making an RC model airplane a vibrant thing of beauty. What a joy to behold, to show and fly. Somehow, after launching such a craft, it seems incredible that your hands could have fabricated and fashioned a device that obeys the laws of nature and conforms to the precepts of engineering—unknown to many but by vague principles—as it performs in accord with your every thought. It is through the handling, control, and observation of model aircraft—along with, hopefully, what I can offer—that vague notions concerning the mechanics of flight (some bordering on folklore) can be cleared up.

DESIGN PARAMETERS

First let's consider some rules of thumb applicable to basic RC airplane design. The wing area, and its thickness and shape (*rib profile*), are governed by the airplane's weight and power. *Wing loading* is the weight, in ounces, carried by each square foot of wing area, a figure which ideally should not exceed 16 ounces per square foot (16 oz/sq ft).

For demonstration purposes, consider an airplane weighing 6 pounds—a good average figure. To derive a figure meaningful for most computations, change pounds to ounces by multiplying by 16: 96 ounces. Now the required wing area can be expressed as:

$$\text{required wing area} = \frac{\text{total plane weight (ounces)}}{\text{optimum wing loading (oz/sq ft)}}$$

$$= \frac{96}{16} \text{ or 6 sq ft}$$

You might have chosen 12 ounces per square foot for a lesser powered craft, for something more of a glider type or one expected to operate at very high altitudes. A heavier wing loading, say, 18 ounces per square foot, would be more suitable for a higher powered, faster airplane (its smaller wing would produce less drag).

We can distribute the area of this wing (6 square feet) by changing its aspect ratio: wing length, or *span* (in inches), divided by *chord* (width in inches).

Usually the greater the aspect ratio, the more efficient the wing—but it also increases drag. Of course, the wing shouldn't be so long and thin that it is structurally weak. Let's continue our calculations.

Six square feet equals 864 square inches: 6×144 (sq in./sq ft) = 864. With a chord of 10 inches (another practical figure), the *wingspan* should be 86.4 inches ($864 \div 10$). Dividing this by 12 (in./ft), we get a span of 7.2 feet. We could have chosen a chord of 12 inches if 7.2 feet was too long for practical purposes, to derive a smaller figure for length or span. Of course, we could have increased the wing loading to 18 ounces per square foot, making the required wing shorter (power would have to be increased, however).

The average fuselage (plane body) is generally about half the length of the wingspan. For our imaginary model, this would be about 3½ to 4 feet. It can be slightly longer than this, say, up to two-thirds the wingspan, and still be all right; in fact, that could give the model greater stability (meaning remaining pointed in the direction of flight, flying right-side-up unless commanded to do otherwise). The fin, or *vertical stabilizer* (sometimes "stab"), the upright part of the tail assembly (to which the *rudder* is attached), should not usually be over 4% of the wing area in size. This is a value proved to be good through experience. The *horizontal stabilizer* (horizontal tail member), to which the *elevator* is attached (to give up and down movement), should be around 10% of the wing area as a general rule. Now the engineering designer might consider such factors as moment arms, forces due to airflow, rib construction, and many other refinements. We won't try to go into these topics here, since they would require another book for their adequate coverage.

We now have some of the general characteristics of an airplane, and a foothold on aerodynamics. The motor for our sample plane would require an engine from 0.45 CID (cubic inch displacement) in size to one with about a 0.61 CID. Larger engines are associated with greater wing loadings. The proper propeller required might range in a size from a 10/6 to a 12/5, the first number in each combination of figures being the length and the second, the distance (in inches) it "screws" forward in one revolution.

FLYING SPEED

One must consider the speed of a model airplane from two points of view: its speed relative to the ground, *ground speed*, and its speed relative to the air around it, *airspeed*. Both contribute to *flying speed*, which can be determined by adding the magnitude and direction (vector) of the factors described. So the air flowing past the plane must be called *relative wind* (Fig. 2-1).

When a model turns to present its side to the wind, its speed must increase to maintain the same lift, because its speed is not directly added to the wind speed. With a sidewind the model may *crab* or turn slightly into the wind, in which case it will not get the same benefit it would from air movement past it as it would flying directly into the wind. Traveling downwind, the velocity (speed and direction) of the air would detract from the model's speed; if the model had a ground speed of 10 mph and the wind was moving at 10 mph in the same direction, there would be no relative airflow and the airplane wouldn't fly.

AERODYNAMIC FORCES

The two primary forces acting on an airplane are *lift* and *drag*. Lift is a force that keeps a plane in the air; drag is the

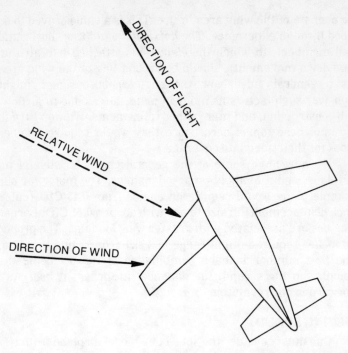

Fig. 2-1. The direction and magnitude of airflow past a wing can only be measured by assuming it is standing still. The two vectors representing the wind's and plane's direction of travel and speed can be combined to find the vector for airflow relative to the plane.

force that resists motion. Lift is produced when the airflow is faster across the top of a wing than under it. This creates a partial vacuum above the wing that allows normal atmospheric pressure below it to hold it up. This can be made to happen by either curving the upper surface so the distance across it is greater, or by inclining the wing at an *angle of attack*. The two types of airfoil we are concerned with are the Clark Y and the symmetrical airfoils shown.

The effect of lift is also used to make a plane bank and turn. When the aileron control is activated to make a plane turn left, the right aileron goes down, while the one on the left is deflected upward; this slows the left wing and increases the lift of the right wing (moving faster than the left wing, it produces more lift), and the plane banks left (Fig. 2-2).

Air behaves like fluids and resists the passage of fast-moving objects through it due to the compression of its molecules. Planes feel the effect of this force too. The force is *drag*. Because drag influences how much power is needed for a plane to fly, and governs its ultimate airspeed, it is important to know how to reduce it for most efficient flight. Drag can have two parts: that part caused by a wing deflecting air; and a part due to turbulent airflow over the body and wing because of protrusions. The turbulence that causes drag in either case has been said to have a "sticky" effect; the turbulent air, in a manner of speaking, sticks to the airplane holding it back. Turbulent airflow just behind the wing, body, and tail occurs around any flat, perpendicular edge protruding there; the partial vacuum created behind them contributes to the effects of drag, which increase with speed. This kind of drag, viscous drag, is only encountered when an airplane is moving relatively fast. It increases directly with the square of the speed.

How do we measure drag? It can be done through the use of a *design number*, one used without units of measure, called the *Reynolds number*. This number is recognized as a statement about how smooth airflow will be over a wing or fuselage, or both. A British physicist, Osborne Reynolds, derived the system using this number when he was trying to find a way to improve the flow of liquids through tubes. A high Reynolds number indicates restricted flow due to turbulence. The *critical* Reynolds number is one just below a value that would indicate drag due to turbulence. For our purposes, Reynolds numbers can be found from the following equation:

$$N_R = VR \times 6.19 \times 10^3$$

In the equation V is the velocity of the wing and R, its chord; the constant was derived from factors of little interest to the

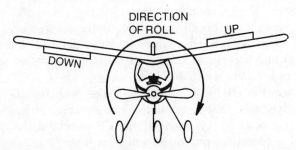

Fig. 2-2. Through the use of linkages, ailerons move in opposite directions to make a plane revolve around its roll axis. A small amount of aileron deflection causes a turn, while a large amount produces a complete roll.

average modeler. Now let's use the equation to test a wing. Suppose the wing in question has a chord of 10 inches and we want to know what to expect from its performance at 50 mph. The information we have must be converted into units used by the equation: 10 inches equals 0.833 feet, $10 \div 12$ (inches per foot); 50 miles equals 240,000 feet, 50×5280 (feet per mile), and 1 hour equals 3600 seconds, 60×60 (seconds per minute times minutes per hour); so 50 mph equals 66.67 feet per second ($240,000 \div 3600$). Substituting, we have:

$$N_R = 66.67 \times 0.833 \times 6.19 \times 10^3$$
$$N_R = 343,769$$

So now that we have a nice large number, what does it mean? Smooth or *laminar* airflow usually occurs around models when the Reynolds number is around 500,000 or less. The value we calculated says that we can expect pretty good performance from the test wing. Actually, for each wing section there is some optimal Reynolds number, but the true performance of a wing can really only be seen in wind tunnels (or during actual flight).

We have considered this important design parameter because when you discuss airplanes with people, the topic of Reynolds number is likely to be mentioned. So you should at least know what it is, its origin, and how it is used. (You probably won't be very concerned with it, especially if building kits that have been engineered for you.)

BALANCE

Next we should examine two very important (although imaginary) points within the mass of an airplane: the *center of pressure* (CP) and *center of gravity* (CG). The center of the lateral area is approximately the center of pressure. The center of gravity is the plane's balance point. The size of vertical and horizontal stabilizers effects the location of the center of pressure. (Fig. 2-3).

When the CP of a model coincides with its CG, it is neutrally stable, that is, it can move to any orientation around these points and stay there. If the CP is behind the CG, a desirable condition, the model will point where it is going like an arrow. If the CP is ahead of the CG, the model might flip nose-over-tail. It is possible to control an airborne object that has its CP ahead of it CG, but control must be constant. Also if

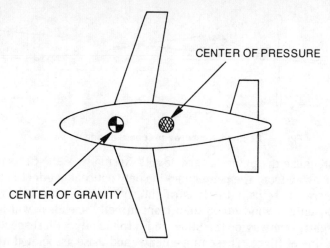

CENTER OF PRESSURE

CENTER OF GRAVITY

Fig. 2-3. Centers of gravity and pressure.

tail surfaces or the fuselage are too short, a model can have its CP in front of its CG. For a highly maneuverable model, the CP should be just slightly behind the CG. For a highly stable model, an attribute needed in areas where crosswinds are a hazard, the CP should be *far* behind the CG; some kit models are built this way. Although we have been talking about the CP being behind the CG, meaning that the center of gravity should be in the cabin area about one-fourth the way back from the leading edge of the wing, and in no circumstances farther back than 1/3 of the chord from the leading edge of the wing when it is mounted on the airplane, there is a small change in the location of the CG of an airplane in flight. This is due to fuel consumption. The CG tends to move back as fuel is consumed, thus making the airplane slightly less stable. Normally this is not a problem. But if you design your airplane for maximum maneuverability, with the CP and CG close to the fuel, the model may become uncontrollable as the fuel is used.

There is much talk about the *centerline* and *thrust line* in model aerodynamics (Fig. 2-4). The thrust line runs through the axis of the propeller. At one time the thrust line was used to counteract the gyroscopic effect of model airplane motors by having it intersect the tip of the vertical stabilizer and located about 3° from the centerline, to the model's right. Modern models use trim controls to adjust for thrust.

Ideally, the CP of an airplane will be located on its centerline. If it isn't exactly on the centerline, torque moments

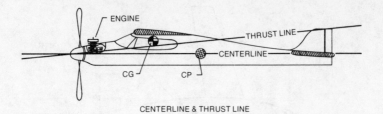

CENTERLINE & THRUST LINE

Fig. 2-4. Relationship between centerline and thrust line.

can cause the plane to turn or roll. Normally, if the CP is not far away from the centerline, the only noticeable effect is the aircraft's refusal to fly straight with some trim; when it encounters wind other than from directly ahead, it will roll slightly one way or the other and turn slightly with respect to its line of flight. These movements, and those associated with normal maneuvers, occur along or around one or more of a plane's three *axes of rotation* (Fig. 2-5), which intersect its CB. A plane banks around its *roll axis*, tilts up or down around its *pitch axis*, and swings left or right around its *yaw axis*. Movement along, rather than around, one of these axes is *transitional movement*, that is, up or down, left or right, forward or backward.

The thrust line may be angled negatively (downward) by 2° or 3° off the centerline so the engine pulls the nose down slightly in flight to compensate for the difference between gliding flight and powered flight. However, with modern RC equipment these differences can be compensated for through trim control. Engines can be made to provide *side thrust* by mounting them so they pull slightly to one side to counteract their gyro effect. Usually the angle is small, 3° to 5°, and depends on the engine size. An airplane tends to rotate in the opposite direction of the propeller's rotation. This slight rotation makes the airplane turn in that direction; in the event of severe rotation—as might be caused by a very powerful engine—a plane would make a turning dive to the ground. But this gyro effect is counteracted for in some models by the side thrust of the engine.

There is a difference between statically balancing a model (at rest) and dynamically balancing it. There is a CG for the wing and the horizontal and vertical stabilizers, but they are not usually specified. These points are combined to locate the final or total balance point of the airplane; it is marked as the

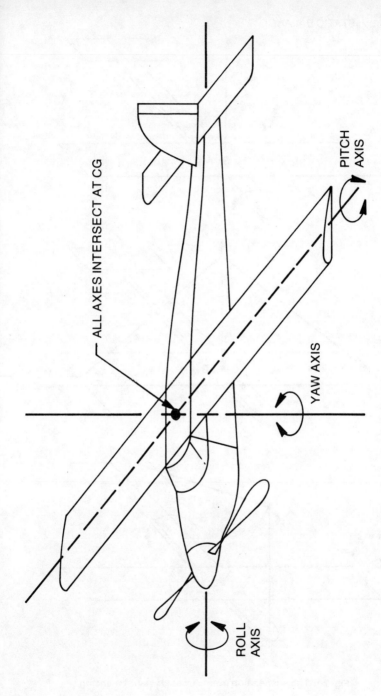

ALL AXES INTERSECT AT CG

PITCH AXIS

YAW AXIS

ROLL AXIS

Fig. 2-5. Axes of rotation.

37

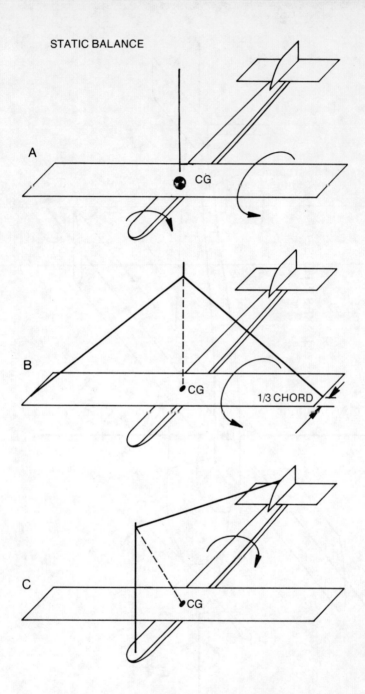

Fig. 2-6. The suspension points used for static balancing.

CG or center of balance. The procedures for static balancing are illustrated in Fig. 2-6; in A, a string is attached to the plane at its CG (with motor in place) to ascertain whether a wing half, the nose, or the tail is too heavy. With strings attached per the example in B, nose or tail heaviness can be seen. In C the string is attached between nose and vertical stabilizer for a display of unbalance in either wing or tail. Dynamic balance (of the plane in flight) compensates for wind forces, uneven lift, and discrepencies in the design CP.

AIRFOILS

Two common *airfoil* (wing) cross sections, or *rib profiles*, are used: the *flat-bottom* type that produces lift even at small negative angles of attack; and the symmetrical or stunt type that must be at a positive angle of attack to produce lift. *Angle of attack* is the angle included between the plane of the wing and the plane of its motion (Fig. 2-7).

One of the best known RC model airplane designers, Claude McCullough of Sig Manufacturing, says the symmetrical airfoil is inherently unstable for models and, thus, they must be under constant control, while configurations like the Clark Y are inherently stable, meaning

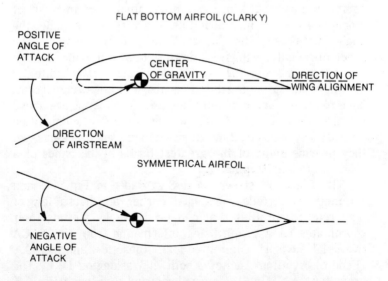

Fig. 2-7. Because a symmetrical airfoil will produce negative lift at a negative angle of attack, it can be used to hold an airplane in the air while it is flying upside-down; it is commonly used for stunt flying.

Fig. 2-8. The Clark Y is an airfoil employed on the Sig Kadet.

the airplane will fly by itself in the absence of control signals. Thus the latter type is easier for a newcomer to handle. *High wing* aircraft are the most stable because their configuration gives a pendulum effect: weight below the wing helps to keep the plane righted. Some years ago the pylon-mounted wing was introduced. A section of the fuselage is built up to hold the wing high above it. Carl Goldberg claims credit for this very stable design, which stirred up a controversy in its day. The cabin-top mounted wing, a configuration seen in a lot of monoplanes, is a stable airfoil using a very obtuse angle: the angle betweeen the wings and the horizontal. The shoulder-mounted wing is set down somewhat into the fuselage but is located above the CG. The *low wing* is attached to the bottom of the fuselage; the CG is above it. Low-wing aircraft have relatively acute dihedral angles: the wingtips are above the aircraft's CG. The latter two types are fast, competition aircraft that need constant attention to prevent crack-ups, yet they provide some of the greatest thrills in the hands of a really proficient RC pilot.

The Clark Y, shown on a Sig. Kadet in Fig. 2-8, and symmetrical airfoils mentioned earlier are but a few of numerous rib profiles that can be drawn by plotting their coordinates on a graph using information from the NACA (National Advisory Committee for Aeronautics) and the FAA (Federal Aviation Agency), both in Washington D. C. The graph for the NACA 6412, a popular airfoil, is shown in Fig. 2-9. In this designation, 6 is a series number; 4, the point of highest camber (45%); and 12, the maximum thickness as a percentage of the airfoil's length. The vertical lines represent percentages of the airfoil chord. To convert these figures from percentages to inches, divide them by 100, then multiply the result by a workable chord. The numbers so derived will give the proper plotting points along the *stations*, horizontal graph lines, and *camber* distances from the baseline. Figure 2-10 shows the points plotted for a 10-inch symmetrical airfoil like that used on the Sig Kougar (Fig. 2-11).

A wing needs to be strong and have spars (lengthwise structural members) thick enough to withstand lift and other forces without breaking during flight. The force distribution on a wing should be such that the greatest lift occurs close to the fuselage, where the wing needs to be thickest. Usually planking and double spar members are used for strength here. The greatest strength along a wing is obtained by making it have a D-shaped cross section. This is done by simply closing in the leading edge (front edge) back to the main spar with balsa planking. The other spars maintain the wing shape, provide warp resistance, and add some strength against lift. Building a glider requires different construction techniques. Glider wings are usually long with narrow chords and use a wedge construction like that seen in building girders. This type of construction gives the necessary strength and rigidity to spars. The covering material for a wing, while it should be smooth enough to give a low Reynolds number, must also afford the wing strength. Some of the new covering materials, such as MonoKote, may fill the bill nicely if they are applied correctly. In some cases, however, incorrect application makes the covering loosen, causing a loss of wing strength and, possibly, producing turbulence. My preference is silk; it shrinks down tightly, providing strength for a wing, tail, or body section. Sometimes a covering is made by applying strong plywood or similar laminations over a plastic foam core.

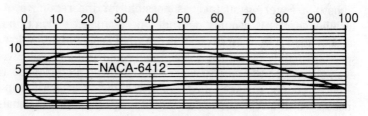

Fig. 2-9. Plot of NACA 6412 airfoil.

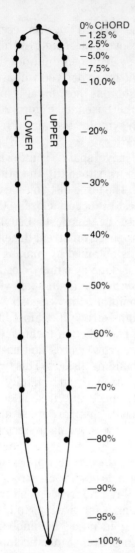

0% CHORD
— 1.25 %
— 2.5%
— 5.0%
— 7.5%
— 10.0%

LOWER UPPER

— 20%

— 30%

— 40%

Fig. 2-10. Plot of NACA 12% symmetrical airfoil.

— 50%

— 60%

— 70%

— 80%

— 90%
— 95%
—100%

Although as an aircraft modeler you should strive for as smooth a covering surface as possible for the reduction of turbulence that would degrade performance, don't be discouraged if your first effort is not what is should be. At low speeds, models classified as *beginners* and *trainers* will fly, even perform quite nicely, when their covering material has a slightly rough surface. Just keep working at it until your models ultimately have a smooth, glossy, professional appearance.

POWER REQUIREMENTS

A plane must have adequate power to maintain controlled flight. The power needed can be calculated once the size of the propeller and its speed of rotation are known. The force a propeller produces to pull an airplane through the air is *thrust*. To stay aloft, the thrust must equal the counteracting force of drag. For an airplane to move forward and increase speeds, the thrust must be greater than the drag. Each change in speed introduces a change in drag; the motor speed must be adjusted accordingly to keep the model moving evenly at each speed. An airplane taking off from the ground must accelerate until it reaches flying speed. This means that the power plant must furnish thrust much greater than the drag for the plane to reach flying speed quickly. Once the plane is airborne, pulling back on the throttle until the thrust is only slightly greater than drag will make it attain level flight. Theoretically, the thrust at this time should be equal to drag, but, practically, it would be just a little greater. Pulling back on the throttle further reduces the thrust so that drag becomes the greater force; the airplane must gain added speed from gravity to keep it flying.

How does one choose the proper power plant for his model? Since an engine's horsepower must move all parts of the plane through the air to overcome drag, and since the wing (the largest part) produces the greatest drag, it is the wing's *coefficient of drag* (available with the design criteria for various airfoils) that must be dealt with primarily:

$$\text{drag} = C_D \ AV^2 \ \times 1.17 \times 10^{-3}$$

Fig. 2-11. In the highly maneuverable Sig Kougar, the CP is close to but behind the CG. The thin horizontal stabilizer reduces drag while providing stability; the wing section can be seen to be fully symmetrical.

In the equation C_D is the wing's coefficient of drag (0.02 for the Clark Y at no angle of attack, for example); A, the wing area (sq ft); and V, the plane's velocity (ft/sec). Multiplying the drag by the plane's velocity in feet per second gives the power required in foot-pounds per second. Since 1 horsepower is equal to 550 foot-pounds per second, we can divide by this number to derive the horsepower required:

$$\text{required horsepower} = \frac{drag \times velocity}{550}$$

The unit of drag, in this case, is pound; for velocity, it's feet per second. Using the value for drag given in the first equation in the second, we have

$$\text{required horsepower} = \frac{C_D\, AV^3 \times 1.17 \times 10^{-3}}{550}$$

$$= C_D\, AV^3 \times 2.13 \times 10^{-6}$$

Notice that horsepower increases as the cube of speed. This means you simply cannot change your engine from a 0.25 CID to a 0.5 CID and expect to double your speed. Let's work out a sample problem now. Assume the airfoil you're concerned with is a Clark Y 6 feet in surface area moving through the air at 44 ft/sec (about 30 mph) and at a 6° angle of attack. What is its drag? How much horsepower is required to maintain this speed at this angle of attack? We can use aerodynamics tables or graphs to find the relationship of the coefficients of lift and drag to the angle of attack for any rib profile. Using such sources we would find that the coefficient of drag for this airfoil at this angle of attack is 0.0452. Now we can calculate the horsepower required:

$$\text{required horsepower} = C_D\, AV^3 \times 2.13 \times 10^{-6}$$
$$= 0.0452 \times 6 \times 44^3 \times 2.13 \times 10^{-6}$$
$$= 0.0492$$

Doubling the speed, you would find the horsepower requirement increased by a factor of eight.

Modern kit models are designed to be used with a recommended range of motor sizes. Usually the smaller the engine within this range, the greater its gyro effect and the less vibration encountered. The power you need must be what you require for your particular situation. In some locations where nice weather prevails, small engines suffice for gliderlike flight. In places where wind is a problem and gusts can appear suddenly, a heavier model with sufficient reserve power (from a larger engine) will be needed. You have to be the judge, perhaps after checking with people in your area, of what your own requirements are. The aircraft you use and its power plant must be tailored to your favorite flying site.

RELIABILITY

Although the topic of reliability might seem somewhat misplaced here, it is an important concept. The probability of equipment's success is the product of the individual components' probability of success. Probability is the term used to state what percentage of the time the device will operate as it should, compared to its down time (the period it is out of service due to a malfunction). If we have five items in a system, say, a transmitter, receiver, servo, motor, and battery—each of which must function correctly for successful airplane operation—and each item has an 80% probability of success (meaning that 80% of the time it works as it should), the overall reliability of the system is the product of five terms; that is $0.8^5 = 33$, or 33%. This *could* mean that one out every three flights would be successful. But, probability being what it is, it could also mean that out of 1000 flights the first 300 or so might be successes, followed by one failure or a series of failures. Usually the first meaning is the one understood: chances are that out of your first three attempts, only one flight will be successful. What, then, is necessary for high reliability, the kind virtually guaranteed by modern model-making methods? The answer is that *each part* must be very reliable. Assuming each part to be 98% reliable, the same type of calculation made previously yields a system reliability of 90%, or 9 successful flights out of 10—pretty good. When you consider the hundreds of little individual parts that make up the present-day RC system, its total reliability is truly amazing.

THE "IDEAL" PLANE

Obviously in referring to the *ideal* model airplane, I can't point to a specific brand, nor even to a specific configuration;

after all, that would put only one kind of plane in the air. My definition of the ideal is actually the average: what is flown most often by the most people; and the one the model enthusiast finds the most practical, the most enjoyable to build, and the easiest to operate. In an effort to describe this craft, I queried modelers throughout the United States. I asked the recipients of my questionnaires what they fly most often, and what is its weight, wing chord, and wingspan, what powers it, and what controls are used. Using the information that came to me, I was able to derive a composite "ideal" airplane that should, theoretically, fly and perform well almost anywhere in the U. S.; regardless of its altitude or prevailing climatic conditions. It should also be relatively easy to build. Although it can't be pictured here, I can at least present its specifications:

WING CHORD	10.5 in.
WINGSPAN	57 in.
WING LOADING	24.1 oz/sq ft
WEIGHT	98.4 oz (6.15 lb)
WING AREA	588 sq in.
ENGINE SIZE	0.45 CID
HORIZONTAL STABILIZER	15.4 % wing area
VERTICAL STABILIZER	7.6% wing area
LENGTH	72% wingspan (propeller to tail)

The largest airplane described was a scale model weighing 12 pounds and having a 1-foot chord and a 94-inch wingspan. If asked to guess, I'd say it was a Taylor Cub. This model, powered by a 0.60 CID engine, seems to be the average used by RC modelers. The smallest airplane (considering only outdoor types) weighs 1½ pounds and has a 16-inch wingspan and a 4-inch chord; the engine was given as 0.049 (CID). Because of its computed wing loading, 54 oz/sq ft, I suspect this airplane is flown with a control line. What seems to be the most reasonable of the smaller planes, and there were many of them, had these specifications: weight, 2.25 pounds; chord, 9 inches; span, 48 inches. Calculations show this model to have a wing loading of only 12 oz/sq ft. This model must surely fly well; so well in fact, it would be a good glider. (That small a model, however, might be tricky to control in a wind.) The average number of controls used is four: motor, rudder, elevator, and aileron.

3

Motors and Props

The modern radio-controlled model airplane's power plant is a scientifically designed engine with a throttle that governs the flow of fuel and air into a venturi (intake port). The fuel and air then pass into the crankcase and then to the piston head where they are burned as a mixture to power the propeller. The engine may have a linkage that controls an exhaust port opening. The 0.4 CID K&B (Aurora Products) engine in Fig. 3-1 has this feature. The engine shown is a little smaller than those most modelers use (according to my survey) but is close enough to represent the average.

FUEL SYSTEMS

Some model aircraft engines use a pressure system fed from the muffler that pressurizes the fuel tank, thereby causing fuel to flow into the engine regardless of the plane's position in flight. There are also engines with a small pump attached to the rear of the crankcase and motivated by the crankshaft, which makes fuel constantly available to the engine. These pressure and pump systems are. for the most part, used in highly maneuverable or high-speed aircraft. The *Sunday flier*, a term for planes flown in the most relaxed manner, has a fuel tank that empties because of suction from the engine. The tank, which is usually plastic, has an air vent so it won't develop a vacuum inside, and a flexible feed line

Fig. 3-1. The dark component in the K& B motor shown is a carburetor; attached to it are two arms, one of which is connected to an exhaust baffle; the other is the attachment point for a servo linkage.

weighted at the end to keep it submerged in fuel no matter what the fuel's position as governed by gravity or centrifugal force. Figure 3-2 shows a typical fuel tank.

Some older airplane models use a tin tank with a slightly rounded V shape (the V's apex pointed downward). The fuel feed line is a copper tube soldered in place so that it almost reaches the back of the tank near the bottom (Fig. 3-3). The fill

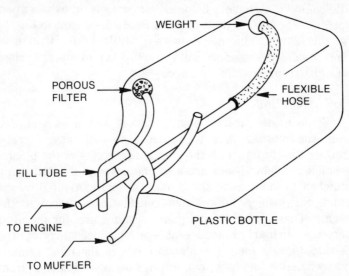

Fig. 3-2. Fuel tanks for RC aircraft come in various sizes. The filter and weight insure proper fuel feed and performance.

and air lines are two small sections of copper tubing soldered in place atop the tank. The advantage of the plastic tank is that during inverted flight, the weight follows the fuel. The V tank's rigid construction prevents this. So the tank you use should be a type that best accommodates the various attitudes your plane is capable of in flight. I like a plastic tank for the positive fuel feed it provides under most flying conditions.

The fuel tank size, its location, and its height in the engine compartment have a great influence on airplane engine operation. The tank should be located close to the engine, it must be vented to the outside (unless pressurized or pumped), and it must be located so that its centerline is ¼- to ⅜-inch below the fuel line connected to the venturi. Sometimes excessive foaming of the fuel due to engine vibration can be alleviated by mounting the fuel tank in form rubber or some other shock-absorbant material, where it can be held in place by rubber bands. I prefer eliminating vibration, if possible, by other means: propeller balancing or other motor mounting methods, for examples.

ENGINE OPERATION

Modern RC model aircraft use two-stroke cycle engines, which, unlike the common Otto four-stroke cycle types found in most cars, combines intake/compression and power/

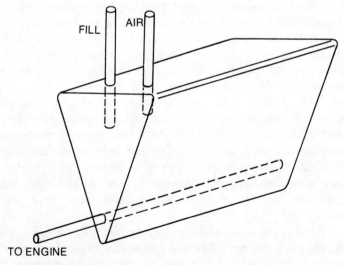

Fig. 3-3. Thin fuel tank with soldered copper lines.

exhaust operations: power is delivered to the crankshaft upon each complete revolution. As the piston approaches its uppermost limit within its cylinder, receiving its motion from a previous explosion of a fuel/air mixture, it compresses a fresh fuel/air mixture into a very small area, in which a glow plug is located (a device much like a spark plug, but requiring no electricity once engine operation has begun). The mixture ignites, driving the piston downward, thus turning the crankshaft to which it is attached by a piston rod. During this *stroke* a port is opened, allowing the escape of burned fuel, now a gas. At this time a vacuum is created at the top of the cylinder that causes fuel and air to be drawn in, after which it is compressed and ignited for the next power/exhaust stroke. The glow plug must be connected to a battery to start the engine; but the residual heat of subsequent power strokes keeps the plug hot enough for engine operation with the battery disconnected.

The components of the exhaust gases expelled are oxidized nitromethane and castor oil, the fuel used; the castor oil lubricates the engine and the nitromethane supplies the power. The residues expelled from the exhaust find their way into the engine compartment (usually) and go over the side of the airplane and under the wing, making a cleanup necessary after each flight—assuming the flier is fastidious in this respect. Glues used in models are usually fuelproof, as is the dope used on the covering material. But you must wipe up and clean off this residue from the exhaust pipe after each flight.

There are many ways in which a motor can be mounted: upright, upside down, or sideways (Fig. 3-4). Whatever its position, the engine should be mounted to hardwood rails, or to metal engine mounts with carbon steel self-locking hex nuts and hardened, steel-alloy machine screws. When you are starting an engine or moving around in front of it, be careful; if you have not mounted the engine securely with fatigue-resistant screws or bolts, it could leave the airplane and seriously hurt you or someone else nearby. I have seen this happen. (Fortunately, only slight injury was sustained by the modeler whose plane was improperly constructed.)

What is the effect of using wood or metal motor mounts on engine performance? The answer seems to be a matter of personal preference. I can only say that the efficiency of an engine depends on the amount of power it transfers to the

Fig. 3-4. Motor and muffler installation in a Sig Kommander. The strap helps to dissipate heat; note the height of the fuel tank relative to the engine position.

propeller. This means that ideally the engine should be rigidly mounted so it can't move when it is turning the propeller. We know this isn't the case. When the engine fires, the propeller tends to stop and the motor tries to turn. In practice this means a very slight amount of power is absorbed by motor mounts not perfectly rigid. Wooden *motor beams* can be anchored with glue back within the fuselage, away from dripping oil and fuel. A radial mount may work itself loose if the firewall it is attached to becomes oil-soaked and gets spongy; but they are easier to install and have been widely used with success.

ENGINE BREAK-IN

There are many pros and cons regarding the issue of engine break-in. I prefer breaking in an engine before flying with it. Besides the obvious advantage in doing this, the rich fuel residue that results when breaking in an engine with a rich fuel mixture can be kept from saturating the airplane. Of

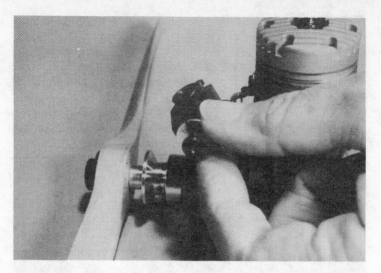

Fig. 3-5. Side view of needle valve adjustment knob. Some modelers solder extensions to the knob so they can make adjustments with their fingers away from the propeller area.

course, you may not have the space or location at home for this kind of bench-testing. But you can break in an engine in an airplane at the flying field; just be careful. If the engine is stubborn in meeting your expectations, as many are during their debut, others will be present who can lend a hand and help you get the reluctant contraption running. This can be a time when you might feel like giving the thing right back to its maker.

When breaking in an engine, use a fuel that contains no more than 10 to 12% nitromethane until the engine has operated several hours. Avoid the use of hot fuels during break-in. Once it's started, run the motor *rich* by adjusting the throttle so that it makes a burbling sound. Now and then you can make the mixture leaner to get the engine going well; don't be concerned about smoke at the exhaust. Use the needle valve adjustment knob shown in Fig. 3-5. Then adjust the throttle so that the fuel/air mixture richens and the engine slows and runs smoothly, throwing out large amounts of castor oil and smokey exhaust. You should not run the engine too long at first; 3 to 5 minutes is enough. Then let it cool off, repeat the procedure until it has about an hour of operating time on it.

An engine will usually be ready for lean operation (full power) after about an hour of break-in. Then you can run it at full throttle with a lean fuel/air mixture for maximum thrust. When the engine holds its speed after the fuel/air mixture has been made lean (you can determine this by listening to the pitch of the engine's sound: you can hear speed changes easily once you get accustomed to listening for them), you can consider the motor broken-in.

I usually test my engines for a couple of minutes at full throttle, and then at various throttle positions. If it responds nicely without gasping, slowing, or choking, I consider it broken-in and adjusted for flight. At times I use an oversize propeller during break-in for greater airflow past the engine, to keep it from running too fast and to provide some turning momentum.

STARTING UP

There are several starting procedures for model airplane engines. Electric starters (Fig. 3-6) are convenience and safety devices that help to make flying RC model airplanes a pleasure. You may also start an engine by hand, flipping the propeller with your fingers; or you may wind the propeller

Fig. 3-6. Using an electric starter. Notice the modeler's grip on the aircraft.

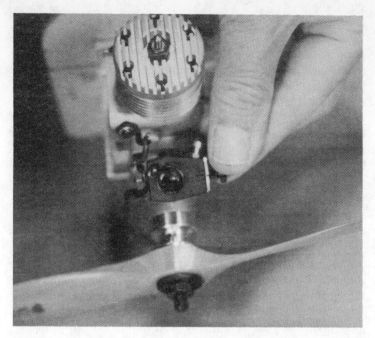

Fig. 3-7. Looking down into the venturi. Adjustment of the fuel/air mixture (rich or lean) is made with the knob at the right.

against a self-contained spring (many tiny motors use a spring system). The following are general steps in the starting procedure (make sure the propeller is on tightly beforehand):

1. When you have put on the propeller, try to adjust its position so that when it is vertical, you feel a definite back pressure (some prefer it horizontal, however). The idea is to have the best position for you when you start to flip the propeller to start the motor. You will be turning it against piston pressure. The propeller's starting position must be such that it allows you to feel comfortable with it: you must be completely relaxed and in control.

2. Turn the needle valve (top view shown in Fig. 3-7) counterclockwise three or four turns from fully closed (fully clockwise position).

3. Place a finger over the open end of the venturi and flip the propeller quickly two or three times; this causes fuel to be sucked in from the tank into the upper part of the piston, priming the motor. You might have to

prime the motor by squirting a little fuel into the open cylinder head to start it sucking properly. But use caution. Too much fuel can cause a flooded condition; too little will starve the engine. You may have to flip the propeller once or twice again; for a "tight" engine, fewer turns may suffice. Do not have the glow plug connected to the battery at this time; you are merely priming the engine, not trying to start it.

4. Carefully connect the booster battery to the glow plug. When the engine starts, the plane may jerk; or you may jerk it involuntarily as the engine fires. In both circumstances, the glow-plug wires may get within the propeller's arc, causing the plane to flip over. Run the wires and make connections to the rear of the glow plug, well back under the wing or over it, so wires cannot possibly get entangled in the propeller when the engine starts.

5. Slowly turn the propeller counterclockwise until you feel a momentary resistance, indicating that the mixture in the cylinder has just fired. This will not be enough to start the engine; it will just cause a resistance to your hand moving the propeller. Now position the propeller and flip it with the tips of your fingers, jerking your hand away with each flip. The motor should start and continue to run. Holding the airplane carefully, get into a position that allows you to adjust the needle valve. Once the engine is running, use the small screw at the side of the venturi to adjust the fuel/air mixture as required for break-in or normal operation. Use care; the stems are close to the propeller's arc. Hold the airplane tightly, as demonstrated by the flier in Fig. 3-8 (notice how he keeps his hands well clear of the propeller), so the motor won't shift position as you adjust the needle valve. Listen to the sound of your engine; you should be able to tell when it reaches its peak speed during the adjustment. Now open the needle valve just a little more, say, two or three "clicks" (fractions of a turn). You won't hear the click; rather, you will feel it as the valve is rotated against the pressure of its leaf spring. This introduces a richer mixture, and will insure that the motor won't stall in flight.

Fig. 3-8. Aircraft must be held tightly when they are started; having an assistant would make the procedure even safer.

6. Operate the throttle with the RC system to see if you have adequate range from high to low engine speeds. If the speed range is satisfactory and easily controllable, you are ready to fly; it not, further adjustment is needed.

It has been reported that certain fuels, often in combination with freak accidents, can cause an engine to run backward: yet another reason to hold an airplane as tightly as possible while starting its engine; the plane may lurch backward and, if you're not prepared for this possibility (supposedly occuring during 2% of all starting attempts), serious injury would be a certainty.

Engines being started in cold weather can be primed with butane, using the canisters intended for cigarette lighters (correspondents have recommended Ronson's Multifill for its easily adaptable valve). To do this, rotate the propeller until the engine sucks some butane into its cylinder, then attach the glow-plug wires and flip the prop as you would for normal starting. Some modelers who fly in cold weather find that they can keep their engines warm between flights by connecting a large nicad (nickel-cadmium) battery to their glow plugs; this makes the engine easier to restart.

To stop your engine you may only have to throttle back completely. Or you may have to throttle back to the slowest speed and then put your finger over the venturi to prevent air from entering. (You must stop feeding fuel to the engine or prevent air from mixing with the fuel.)

ENGINE CARE

Here are some tips for the care of your engine:

- Always provide for good airflow around your engine. It is air-cooled and must not be tightly enclosed unless some means of cooling it is provided (such as a fan attached to the shaft).
- It may be necessary to use an air filter (obtainable from your hobby dealer or the engine manufacturer) if you live in a dusty area.
- Keep your engine clean externally by wiping it with solvent using a rag or brush, or use a liquid formulated for this purpose. A buildup of dirt and oil can raise the engine's operating temperature beyond a safe limit. You can judge the operating temperature by fastening a piece of 50-50 solder to the central cooling fin of your engine's cylinder head. If it melts, the engine's temperature is above 400°F, too hot: greater airflow is needed around it, or heat sinks must be added.

The most basic problems with engines are improper fuel/air mixtures (improper needle valve adjustment), poor ignition (faulty plugs), worn carburetors, and insufficient compression. These are causes of hard starting, loss of power, slow throttle response, and unreliable engine performance. Some motor problems and their remedies follow:

- Improper fuel/air mixtures are caused by the improper placement of fuel tanks, poor fuel-tank design, incorrect needle valve adjustment, kinked or plugged fuel lines, leaky connections, or a fouled fuel vent.
- Poor ignition may be caused by a weak or worn battery, a worn, defective, or inappropriate glow plug,

and poor connections between battery and glow plug, including broken wires, dirt preventing positive contact, shorted terminals at the glow-plug connector, or a leak at the glow-plug gasket.

- Compression should be felt as a resistance to turning the propeller with the engine off and cool. If you do not feel this resistance, suspect a leaky cylinder, a loose or defective glow plug, or a worn or loose cylinder head gasket. Or the engine may be worn out, requiring new rings and seals, etc.

- If the engine speed varies (even though you are not applying throttle), there may be a leak in the crankcase. This might have been caused by a bad landing or other impact. A pinhole in the fuel line or a loose hose connection may also cause this problem. Disconnect the booster battery and make certain that no sparking or arcing occurs while the motor is running; arcing can be the source of electrical interference causing the motor control servo to react in a random erratic manner. Inspect the servo (with the battery disconnected) if radio control of the motor is unsatisfactory.

Once the engine is adjusted and you think it's running properly, adjust the throttle for high speed, lift the airplane, and point its nose straight up. If the motor continues to run without problems, point the nose straight down and see if the engine works okay in that position. Change the speed to idle and repeat the process. If the motor works okay under these conditions, you should have no trouble in flight. Manufacturers say that if the engine stops when the plane's nose is up, the fuel/air mixture is too lean; if it stops with the plane's nose down, the mixture is too rich. The line drawing of a Perry carburetor in Fig. 3-9 shows all the parts normally found in model engine carburetors and the adjustments possible. The idle-mixture disk regulates the idle mixture—a very sensitive adjustment.

To check your glow plug, simply remove it from the engine and connect it to the battery; if it glows, it's good. However, I have had a glow plug operate properly when tested in this manner, yet, when replaced in the engine, refused to fire. I found out later—after much frantic rechecking—that one end of the glow-plug coil was loose; it was not welded to the plug

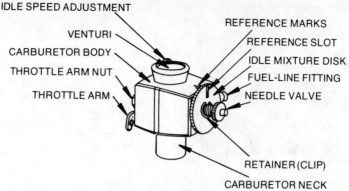

IDLE SPEED ADJUSTMENT

VENTURI

CARBURETOR BODY

THROTTLE ARM NUT

THROTTLE ARM

REFERENCE MARKS

REFERENCE SLOT

IDLE MIXTURE DISK

FUEL-LINE FITTING

NEEDLE VALVE

RETAINER (CLIP)

CARBURETOR NECK

Fig. 3-9. Carburetor by Perry Aeromotive.

contacts as it should have been. When the engine was still, or when the plug was out of the engine, the coil touched the contacts and burned brightly. But, when I tried to start the engine, the end would jar loose, the coil would cool off, and the engine remained dormant. Finally, with a new glow plug I succeeded. The moral: When in doubt, replace the glow plug.

I have been told by a few that the main reason for modeler's troubles with their products is an unwillingness to read and follow instructions (the same reason other hobby-oriented manufacturers are plagued by unfounded complaints). Some people skim over instructions, and then do what they *think* the instructions said. Others glance at the instructions and assume they understand what is being said, based on previous experience with a similar system. Reading instructions should be a systematic process. Read them carefully and underline important words and phrases; think over what has been said and see if you can repeat it, either to yourself or someone else; read the instructions again to verify your interpretation. This could take more time than you would want to devote to instructions. I have to force myself to consider each word, reading the instructions at least three times with pencil in hand, making sure I don't skip words or phrases. I also make certain I understand what the words mean, that I don't skip some words because I don't understand them.

MUFFLERS

One respondent to my questionnaires made a comment about mufflers, a recurrent comment made by many: "Use

Fig. 3-10. Kraft 0.61 (CID) engine with muffler.

them and avoid trouble." Some model clubs have voted to require mufflers on their models (one can be seen in Fig. 3-10, upper left), but a muffler may not reduce noise to an acceptable level. A representative of one club said they wanted engine noise reduced by 3 decibels.

The sound of an engine can be measured by the decibel. A term first used by the Bell Telephone Company to specify the sound level of telephone conversations, *decibel* (abbreviated dB) is a unit expressing the ratio of two amounts of electric or acoustic power:

$$dB = 10 \, Log_{10} \, \frac{P_2}{P_1}$$

P_1 is a lesser power being compared to a greater power, P_2. For our purposes the booklet obtainable from the Academy of Model Aeronautics concerning noise and its legal aspects is a worthwhile publication to write for. Some of the clubs I contacted have established a 90 dB limit on engine noise (without mufflers) and police themselves with the aid of a sound-level meter. Their established limit is a good one to strive for; sound levels of 120 dB can be painful—literally. With mufflers, the 90 dB engine noise level can be reduced by 3 dB (changes in sound level of 1 dB are just discernible to the ear). Unfortunately, most muffler manufacturers do not specify noise reduction in dB for their products.

There are alternatives to reciprocating engines for model airplanes: jet and electric engines. Although experimentation with pulse jets for models is underway, their high noise output makes them, for the time being, impractical for most areas. Electric motors, on the other hand, have a lot going for them: they produce less vibration than their fossil-fueled counterparts, and the sound they emit—a mere whisper compared to the screams of their reciprocating cousins. Their only drawbacks are high current demand leading to rapidly depleted batteries and overheating on long flights. But by using nicad batteries, an electric-powered plane can achieve a respectable flight duration if taken to an altitude from which it can soar with its motor off. If your takeoff space is limited, if you've been getting complaints about noise—look into electric-powered planes.

PROPS

The motor manufacturer will recommend the appropriate propeller size. You could also find out what propeller sizes other hobbyists in your area are using on the same size engine. You may need to balance your propeller. Hobby shops can supply the tool needed: a spindle to mount the propeller on. Try to adjust the balance, perhaps by shaving a little off one tip or the other so neither is heavier; using the spindle you can set the prop in any position without it rotating a heavy side downward.

It now seems wise to mention the problems of nicked or broken propellers due, in the main, to less than perfect landings. "Props" get nicked, split, and broken sometimes so slightly that these dings and minor fractures go unnoticed. Sometimes even noticed, damaged props go into service. This can lead to other problems. Although most RC equipment aboard a plane is mounted so as to be isolated from normal vibration, the plane's manufacturer seldom provides for the extra vibration caused by a bad prop, the slower, erratic kind of vibration that can affect RC equipment. So keep an eye on the condition of your prop, and never take chances with a bad propeller or a bent or misaligned spinner.

It has been determined that a low-pitched propeller—*pitch* being the distance a prop would screw forward in a solid—will accelerate faster (get up to speed faster) than high-pitched types but will have a slower top speed. Usually a larger diameter propeller will be more efficient in converting engine horsepower into thrust than a shorter one (that is, shorter in diameter). For the radio control of a normal (as oppossed to racing) airplane, a long propeller with a relatively small pitch is desirable.

Altitude can make a difference in propeller selection. Where one propeller may work well with your engine at one flying site, at another altitude it may prove unfit. If you travel around the country to attend flying meets, take pains to determine what propeller is most efficient at the sites for each; the prop you've been using with success at home could spell failure in new territory.

Propellers are available in nylon, plastic, and wood. I like wood ones best; they are stiffer than other types and their weight gives momentum to the engine much like a flywheel would.

4

Electronics
for the Modeler

One fact uncovered by my survey is that very few RC
enthusiasts like building electronic equipment from scratch as
part of their hobby. However, a large number do build RC kits
and get good results with them. Most people do not want to
spend a lot of time adjusting electronic hardware once it is
assembled—they want to build and fly airplanes.

But the more you know about something, the better the
results you can obtain from it. Knowing why an automobile
needs oil and water makes a driver more attentive to these
necessities, and thus he receives greater pleasure from his
motoring. Knowledge and diligence pay off in performance
and reduced maintenance. And so it is with RC flying. The
material in this chapter is concerned with the workings of RC
electronics—its function and operation—descriptions and tips
that will help you know what's happening in your gear and
why, and how to make it give long, satisfactory service.

THE ESSENTIALS

It is not necessary for the average modeler to think of his
equipment in terms of resistors, capacitors, inductors—the
bits and pieces that comprise circuits; nor is it even
worthwhile considering transistors and other solid-state
devices. In the equipment we intend to use, these have been
incorporated into modular electronic building blocks—whose

function *is* our interest. Without knowing what the innards of our cars' carburetors look like, we know when they're flooded and, sometimes, what to do about it. Analogous situations arise with RC equipment; it's those situations you should be able to cope with.

The most prominent of the building blocks are amplifiers. But we can't discuss them without some backtracking to the basics of electricity because saying *amplifier* immediately raises the query, amplify what? Well, *signals*. Okay, where do these signals come from? At this point, talking about voltage and current is unavoidable. Voltage is a potential for the flow of electricity just as a dammed water reservoir has a potential (has pressure) for water flow. Although capacitors can have a *voltage potential*, the pertinent component here is the battery. When its terminals are connected, its potential starts to diminish; similarly, the water reservoir would loose its potential for water flow were its water to be released. Or the water could be directed in such a way that it does work: turn waterwheels to mill grain, for example. What flows from one battery terminal to the other when both are connected, *current*, can also be used to do work by routing it through the various devices found in electronic *circuits*; the "plumbing" that channels the flow of current: *conductors*; "leaks" are prevented with *insulators*. Circuits in which current flow has been interrupted because of a break (broken conductor, for example) are *open circuits*; those that aren't operating because they have been bypassed have been *short-circuited*. More often than not, the *chassis* upon which the components of a transmitter or receiver are mounted are used as a conductor; connections to this conductor are *ground* connections. The analogy between electricity and water, and the two's behavior, is a good one. In fact, the British call vacuum tubes *valves*, an apt choice of words because, indeed, vacuum tubes are to electricity what valves are to water: they control its flow.

RC AMPLIFIERS

Amplifiers can convert low-signal inputs to high-signal outputs, the signals either being in the form of voltage or current at either "end" of the device. The transistor, an electronic valve like the vacuum tube, is a current amplifier. The power it controls comes from sources like batteries or power supplies. The ratio of output to input (in current or voltage) is the *gain* of the amplifier. The more sensitive the amplifier, the greater its gain and the smaller the input voltage or current required. Modern receivers can contain amplifiers with a gain of millions, causing them to respond to electrical interference, such as sparking from motors, etc. These unwanted signals can seriously disrupt RC communications.

There are many kinds of amplifiers, each named for its function. Very broadly, amplifiers are classified as either audio- or radio-frequency types (AF or RF types). *Frequency*, in this context, refers to current being switched on and off or reversed in direction at a given rate. The measure of frequency, at one time *cycles per second*, is Hertz (abbreviated Hz; 1 Hz indicates one pulse or one change in current direction per second). AF amplifiers are used with relatively low-frequency sources, even DC (direct current): uninterrupted current flowing in one direction. The subject being radio control, it's RF amplifiers that concern us most.

RF amplifiers are used in RC transmitters and receivers. In the transmitter they are used to amplify control signals so they can be electromagnetically propagated and received. Receivers use an RF amplifier to detect a transmitter's output and convert it to a form that can be used by a servo to move control surfaces on a model plane.

PULSE-FRAME COMMUNICATIONS

Radio-control systems deal with signal codes; codes that must be processed by specialized amplifiers to operate motors for airplane control. *Adding amplifiers* produce an output only when two or more special inputs are present. *Subtracting amplifiers* produce an output proportional to the difference between two input signals. *Comparison amplifiers* are similar to subtracting amplifiers but produce an output that is not only proportional to the difference between two input signals, they also indicate, by output polarity, which input is the greatest. They are also capable of an output proportional to the duration of each signal, and will show which of two signals lasts longest and the difference between their durations.

The signal codes processed by these amplifiers are in the form of pulses. If we were to switch a battery's voltage off and on, we could create voltage pulses. The same principle applies

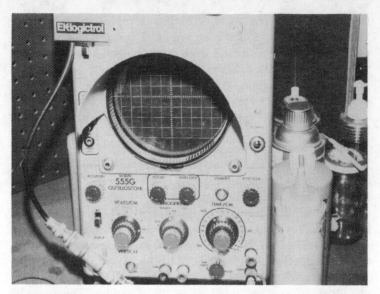

Fig. 4-1. Oscilloscope used at an RC equipment plant. Note the horizontal and vertical zero-reference lines intersecting the center of the CRT's screen.

to the RC transmitter. It is turned off and on by means of an encoding amplifier called a *modulator*, which is essentially an electronic switch that causes the transmitter's carrier (signal) to be regularly interrupted. The manner in which these signal interruptions are varied makes up the code that tells receiving equipment in the airplane what to do: which control to activate, how much to move it, and in what direction.

We cannot see or hear the pulses sent by the transmitter, but we can see them as they are received using an *oscilloscope* (Fig. 4-1), a test instrument with a CRT (cathode-ray or "picture" tube) on which can be displayed the output or condition of a circuit. An oscilloscope can show current and voltage waveforms (Fig. 4-2), which appear across the CRT in a position relative to a zero-reference centerline representing an absence of polarity. Tracings seen above the line are relatively positive and those below the line, relatively negative. An oscilloscope is required to inspect what is happening inside a radio-control transmitter or receiver. An inspection of waveforms can reveal whether equipment is operating incorrectly and, if so, which of its circuits is faulty. Figure 4-3 shows a technician making a repair to a

66

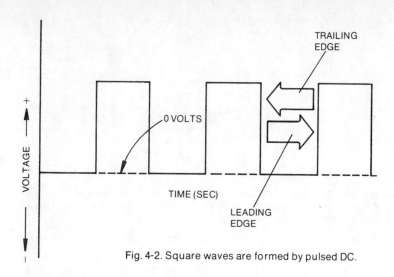

Fig. 4-2. Square waves are formed by pulsed DC.

transmitter, using information displayed on the "scope." Oscilloscopes are of interest to us because they can show us what pulsed RC signals look like: *frames* of square-wave pulses. A frame (sometimes *train*) of square-wave pulses, for our purposes, is of five to eight pulses generated in a series and

Fig. 4-3. Technician making a bench repair to a transmitter. What looks like a large, open-ended coffee can to his left is an antiglare hood on an oscilloscope.

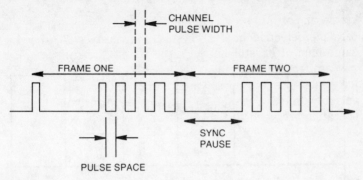

CHANNEL
PULSE WIDTH

FRAME ONE

FRAME TWO

SYNC
PAUSE

PULSE SPACE

Fig. 4-4. The width of each channel pulse may be varied independently. Each pulse goes to a distinct control channel: to a rudder servo, for example; changes in pulse width would turn the rudder.

separated by uniform time increments when no control signal is being transmitted (Fig. 4-4).

Moving a control lever on an RC transmitter changes the pulses' off and on time, making them vary in width (as viewed on a "scope") and duration. These variations are compared to a reference signal generated within the receiver and determine how much a control moves, and its direction of movement. The selection of aircraft controls (by a *channel*) is governed by which pulse in the frame is varied from its normal width and spacing. The spacing between frames is greater than the spacing between pulses. This sync pause permits the onboard equipment to reset, ready for the next frame. When transmitted pulses appear to have the right shape, size, spacing, and intensity, the RC system will operate as it should. If the pulses fail to meet the required specifications, wave-shaping amplifiers have to be employed.

The servo motors within the plane will continue to move between pulse frames due to their momentum; besides insuring uninterrupted operation, momentum prevents the motors from being influenced by occasional random pulses that might get into the system. Some of my respondents have reported that the arcing within high-voltage automobile ignition systems (DC pulses) can be received by RC equipment. The range of these pulses is usually short; sometimes a change in flying site or finding the culprit car can solve the problem.

CHANNELS OF OPERATION

The transmitter (Fig. 4-5) and receiver contain crystal oscillators; both have similar purposes. The transmitter's is to

68

create and amplify a frequency-stable signal through the use of a piezoelectric quartz crystal; the receiver's, using the same kind of crystal on the same frequency (in a matched transmitter/receiver pair), insures that signals on a specific frequency are only received. Thus, neither unit must be variably-tuned to be put "on frequency." If new channels of operation are needed, the units can be returned to the maker for crystal replacement, where they can also be adjusted for maximum output and sensitivity at the new frequency. One manufacturer offers plug-in modules that permit the user to make these changes at home or in the field.

Antennas are critical to a transmitter's or receiver's efficiency. Their length is an important consideration for greatest output and sensitivity and, for this reason, must always be fully extended for reliable communications. If a transmitter's antenna is only partially extended, it cannot effectively radiate its signal to the air; rather, the signal will be dissipated as heat, causing the batteries to drain faster.

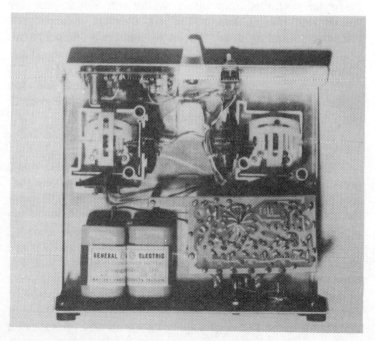

Fig. 4-5. Inside view of a transmitter showing control-stick gimbals (upper right and left) and nickel-cadmium batteries (lower left).

WHAT TO BUY

The number of people that responded to my survey, when multiplied by their individual years of experience in this hobby, represents an almost staggering amount of knowledge. Their tips on buying RC systems must be recounted here. Unanimously, they recommended buying the best you can afford and avoid bargain equipment that can be costly in the long run and will, in any case, give you a poor return on its price when it comes time to sell it. Find out if the manufacturer has a reputation for service, good customer relations, and for making a reliable, high-performance product. If you can't afford the best in new equipment, get the best in used. When buying a kit, check the instruction manual—even though the manufacturer's designers may be top-notch, his editor could be mediocre.

My respondents were also opinionated on the issue of multichannel capability; most were emphatically in favor of four- or five-channel capability (five channels being of special interest to competition fliers). The control channels needed, in the order of importance given by the respondents, are for rudder and motor (the minimum), elevator, aileron, and retractable landing gear. Of course, additional channels can provide control of onboard photographic equipment, flaps, "bomb" release, and so forth.

Buying RC equipment is like buying anything else; the manufacturer's reputation, the equipment's service record, word-of-mouth advertising—these are the best guides.

WEAR AND TEAR

Since electronic equipment depends on current following a predetermined path (circuit continuity), it is obvious that roadblocks in these paths—open or short circuits—will make the circuit malfunction, in turn affecting the operation of the equipment—probably next to battery problems, the RC modeler's most formidable nemesis. Commonly, circuits are made inoperative by fouled switch contacts. Switches are often mounted on airplanes where they are exposed to the risk of fuel residue seeping inside them. Add a small amount of dirt, and you have trouble: the switch becomes incapable of closing the circuit or does so only intermittently (dirt is not a good conductor of electricity). You can check a suspect switch by bypassing it. Connect a short length of wire—or another switch—across it, that is, between the same terminals. If this solves the problem, the switch needs replacing. When building airplanes it is wise to place switches where they are safe from contamination, and where vibration can't affect their making positive contact.

The contacts in switches will wear out through repeated operation. The same is true of connectors and connecting cables. Connectors that are taken apart and put together hundreds of times gradually wear and become loose where they are joined. Cables that are stretched, twisted, and bent continually will eventually break. (Wire breaks inside the insulation cannot be seen.) Try to locate connectors and cables where they are least likely to move. Some motion is all right, but don't place them where they can flop around in flight. And try to make connector joints tight. Always use extreme care when taking connectors apart or putting them together. Don't twist them from side to side; this could enlarge the holes and bend the contact pins inside. And don't take them apart any more than you need to.

HOME REMEDIES

What can you do, not being a technician, to check the condition of your radio-control system? I suggest you get a small volt-ohmmeter (VOM). With it you can measure battery voltage and verify circuit continuity, even in the field. The meter should be at least a 1000-ohms-per-volt type, although 5000 ohms per volt is better. Learn how to use it and read it. Instructions are usually furnished with these instruments. The meter is actually a two-in-one instrument: a combination ohmmeter/voltmeter. The ohmmeter part is used to test continuity and measure resistance (the property of resisting current flow). Its most important application (to you, a modeler) is in checking connectors and cables for continuity. Cables have inner and outer conductors that provide outgoing and return paths between the equipment they connect. Each path must be continuous for the interconnected equipment's proper operation. To check a cable, first turn the meter function knob to OHMS. Touch a test lead (supplied with the meter) to each end of one cable conductor. Full deflection of the meter indicates almost no resistance at all—good conductivity: next, check the other conductor. It is possible that you can get full meter deflection checking the conductors in this way and still have a bad cable: the inner and outer conductors could be making contact. The final check, then, is to touch test leads to both conductors. Here, you are looking for no meter deflection meaning almost infinite resistance or no conductivity.

The voltmeter part of the VOM is useful for determining the condition of a battery. Some people check the individual cells of their batteries (having a *load*, or resistance, connected to it for normal drain). Although charger/discharger systems may tell you if a battery is good or bad, they will not indentify individual defective cells; but a volt-ohmmeter will. Small VOMs are inexpensive and can be used to check other items of equipment as you gain experience in electronics.

5

Transmitters
and Receivers

In this section we examine in detail the operation of radio-control transmitters, which, between different makes, all share the same basic operation. Except for some slight differences in circuitry and control-pulse timing, you could consider them as having come from the same source. I discovered that many of the basic components—integrated circuits, servos, etc.—are foreign-made; one manufacturer stated that some of his parts come from Spain, some from Japan, some from Taiwan, and some from Mexico. The parts are partially assembled when they arrive in the United States, where final assembly and checkout take place. Some manufacturers rely completely on U. S. parts and labor, while others offer equipment assembled and checked outside of the United States.

CONTROLS LAYOUT

The transmitter shown in Fig. 5-1 can be considered typical in its layout and operation. Moving the right-hand control stick (one of two surrounded by square bezels) has a correlative effect on the plane being controlled. Moving it up (elevator control), makes the plane climb; likewise, moving it to the left (rudder control), directs the plane to bank left, and so forth. The extent of the plane's maneuver is controlled directly by the extent of control-stick movement. The stick's

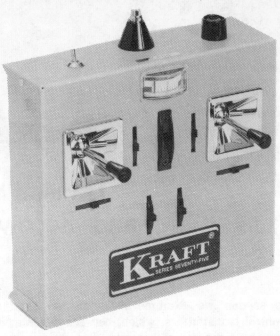

Fig. 5-1. The example for an explanation of RC transmitter operation: the Kraft series 75.

gimbal mounting allows it to be moved in any direction, and by any amount; springs attached to the stick mechanism cause it to return to a neutral position when released.

The left-hand stick, used for throttle and aileron control, is similar in operation to its mate but usually has no return spring. This arrangement permits the throttle to be set and maintained at one position for a steady plane speed. Usually, down is for idle or low throttle and up for full throttle (maximum engine speed). Many modelers prefer to have the rudder and aileron functions reversed from the position described. This can be done at the factory when you order your equipment or, if you are building a Heath system, you can arrange it this way during construction. The arrangement you use will depend on what you find to be most natural for your hand and finger movements; a left-handed person may find the reversed positioning most comfortable.

The rotary controls immediately surrounding the control sticks are used to calibrate the transmitter for neutral flight when the sticks are in the neutral position; these are the *trim tabs*. If your airplane required a little up elevator to fly level, instead of having to hold the stick slightly above the central position constantly, you can position the trim tab so that when level flight is attained, the control stick is in neutral. This same trim idea applies to the other controls: rudder, aileron, and motor. The motor control trim tab will usually adjust the low-idle speed.

A power switch is mounted directly below the meter; below that are two optional channel controls—for flaps or retractable landing gear, for example.

ENCODING

Now let's see what happens when the antenna is extended and the transmitter is turned on with all the controls in the neutral position. Turning on the transmitter starts a *multivibrator* that pulses DC to an encoder in the form of regular, timed *frames* (see Chapter 4). The encoding section is made up of one-shot multivibrators, one for each control channel (Fig. 5-2). When control channel one's half-shot multivibrator receives its pulse, it interrupts the output of the RF section for a specific time, after which it returns to its normal state and triggers channel two's one-shot multivibrator, and so on.

The modulator (shown) is the unit that actually shuts down the RF section during off pulses. It amplifies the pulses and applies the result to a part that causes voltage to be removed from a stage of the RF section. The interruption of this voltage and, consequently, the interruption of the carrier (transmitted signal), is *modulation*.

In the diagram the RF section can be seen to be made up of three blocks or stages: OSC (oscillator), BUFF (buffer), and

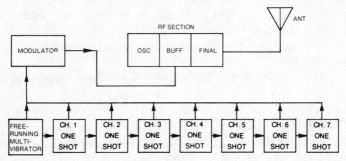

Fig. 5-2. Block diagram of a seven-channel transmitter.

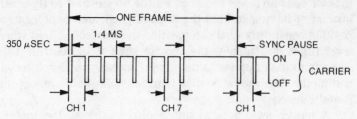

Fig. 5-3. Complete and partial control-pulse frames. Sometimes called trains, these pulse groupings modulate the transmitter's carrier.

FINAL. The oscillator, using a piezoelectric quartz crystal, controls the frequency of the carrier. Its output is matched to the final stage for amplification by the buffer stage; the final stage builds the signal to the strength needed for its radiation as radio waves.

A *sync pause* follows the operation of the last control channel's one-shot multivibrator; its duration, longer than the interval between RF pulses, allows the receiver to reset in preparation for the next pulse frame. Figure 5-3 is a representation of RC information being transmitted. The square waveforms, one for each control channel, represent pulsed RF energy and are separated by narrow off pulses, the first in each series marking the beginning of a pulse frame. Each narrow pulse and its neighboring broader pulse can be considered collectively as a cycle, in this case, one every 1.4 msec (1.4 milliseconds; 1 msec = 0.001 sec).

Remembering that the conditions described so far exist when all transmitter controls are in their neutral position, let's see what happens when a control stick is moved up slightly. The duration of RF pulses changes; instead of a 1.4 msec space between off pulses, it might now be 1.1 msec. The receiver could interpret this change to mean, say, make the servo motor of the elevator channel move the elevator slightly (*slightly* because the spacing of the channel one pulse changed only slightly).

Moving the control stick down causes the second off pulse to be delayed; the transmitter is on channel one longer than normal, say, for 1.6 msec. (The pulse has been widened.) The receiver will interpret this to mean that the servo motor of the elevator channel should move the elevator in the opposite direction, past neutral (1.4 msec pulse). It will stay there as long as the control stick is held down.

Any change in the position of the control stick changes the time at which the second off pulse appears; this is how information is transmitted. Since there are more off pulses per pulse frame than on pulses, and since each appears on time relative to the one preceding it, we can have four, six, eight, or more channels of information, each completely independent of the others. Each successive channel works like the first described. Channel two measures the time between off-pulses two and three; channel three, the time between off-pulses two and three; channel three, the time between off-pulses three and four, etc. When the last channel is reached, the last off pulse starts the sync pause interval, during which no information is transmitted. The carrier remains on, however, blocking out radio noise that might otherwise cause the receiver to behave erratically. The differences between one manufacturer's equipment and another's are in the durations of the on and off pulses, and of the sync pause. The sample pulse frame illustrated is that of a Kraft system; that of Heath equipment is shown in Fig. 5-4A. (Figure 5-4B shows control channel two being activated.)

Looking inside the encoder/modulator of an RC transmitter would reveal little of its operation. You might see a regular arrangement of transistors and suspect them of

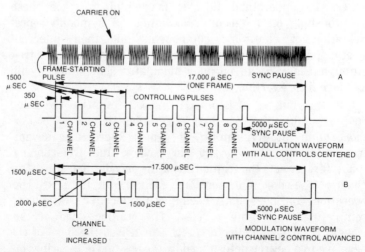

Fig. 5-4. With all controls in the neutral position, Heath equipment's pulse-spacing is 1500 μsec (A); moving a transmitter control changes pulse spacing for one control channel (channel two in B, for example).

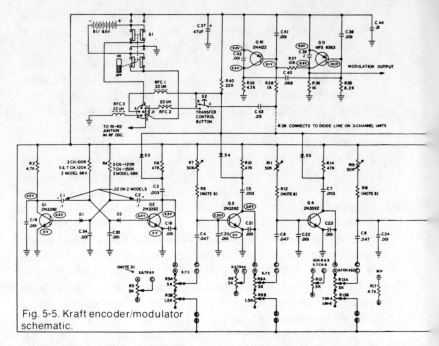

Fig. 5-5. Kraft encoder/modulator schematic.

being the one-shot multivibrators used to generate control
pulses— and you'd be right. But you still wouldn't know how
they are interrelated, how they function in concert with each
other. To understand this, it is helpful to trace these
relationships on a circuit *schematic*: a symbolic representation of electronic components and their interconnecting paths. If you've had experience in this endeavor, a trek
through Fig. 5-5, an encoder/modulator schematic, should
produce little exertion.

In this unit, transistors Q1 and Q2 comprise the free-
running multivibrator that operates the one-shot or
monostable multivibrators, of which there are seven:
transistors Q3 through Q9. In review, the free-running
multivibrator sets the frame rate of the encoder and starts the
chain of one-shot multivibrators, each driving the next. The
operation continues until each has produced its off pulse,
completing the frame (cycle). The trailing edge of the
waveform at Q2's collector (Fig. 5-6) drives the base of Q3
negative to a degree determined by the position of the wiper on
R5 (set by a control stick). C4 starts charging through R7 and
R8 toward the positive voltage supply level until the 6-volt

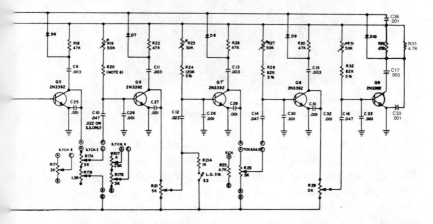

turn-on voltage of Q3 appears at its base. This voltage returns the collector potential to near ground level. The trailing edge of Q3's collector pulse makes Q4 operate in the same manner that the pulse from Q2's collector made Q3 operate when it received a potential at its base.

The serial operation continues from Q4 to Q5, Q5 to Q6, and on through Q8 to Q9. The operation stops until restarted by the free-running multivibrator's frame-starting pulse. The time between these chain actions is the duration of the sync pause, which allows the receiver decoder system to reset for successive chain operations.

Now examine how the RF section is modulated. Connected to each collector of the transistors in the timing chain is a differentiator (C5 and R10) with the anode of diode D4 connected between them. When a sharp pulse appears across the resistor, the diode permits only its negative portion to pass to the base of Q10 through current-limiting resistor R38. Notice that transistors Q10 and Q11 also form a monostable multivibrator. This means that it will cycle once for each negative input pulse. This multivibrator has a long period of operation—300 to 400 μsec (300 to 400 microseconds, 1 μsec

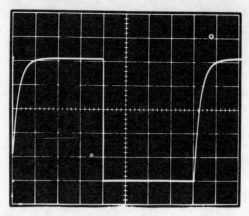

Fig. 5-6. Waveform at the collector of Q2, one of a pair of transistors comprising the free-running multivibrator of the Kraft system.

being 10⁻⁶ second)—which is determined mainly by the value of R35 and C40. The waveform at the base of Q10 is shown in Fig. 5-7A; the waveform at the collector of Q11 can be seen in Fig. 5-7B. The output of Q11, an off pulse, goes to ground (zero voltage level) from the supply. voltage level. Thus it can be seen that if the supply voltage point is connected to the buffer stage of the transmitter, each time the pulse causes the voltage to go to zero, it turns the transmitter's signal off. This is the modulator for the transmitter. The modulated signal is a series of carrier pulses whose width (duration) varies according to the timing of the one-shot multivibrators; their timing is governed by various control stick and lever positions.

The transmitter RF sections for the three frequency bands of operation (27, 53, and 72 MHz) are very similar three-stage

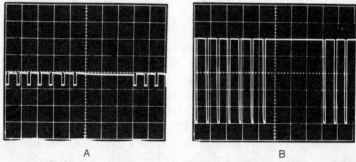

A   B

Fig. 5-7. The waveform at the base of Q10 (A) becomes the waveform at the collector of Q11 (B).

units (Fig. 5-8). They are crystal-controlled and have antenna-matching networks.

Let's compare the operation of the Kraft system to that of a Heath unit. The schematic in Fig. 5-9 is for a 1974 factory-assembled unit, later versions of which are now available as kits. In this transmitter, the free-running multivibrator is composed of transistors Q1 through Q4 and their associated circuitry.

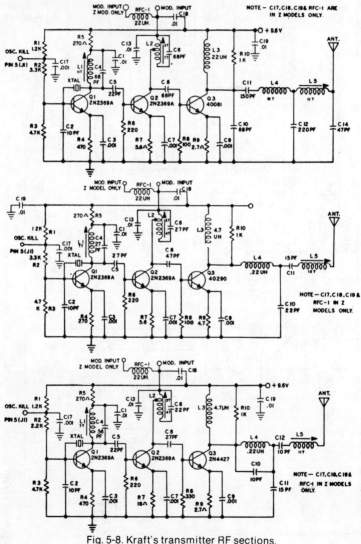

Fig. 5-8. Kraft's transmitter RF sections.

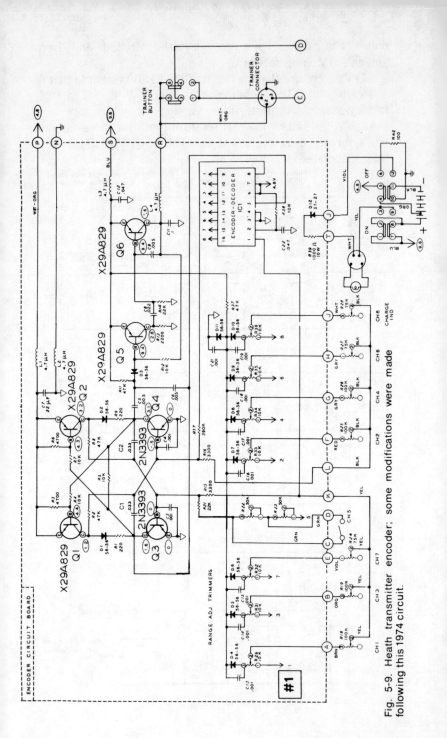

Fig. 5-9. Heath transmitter encoder; some modifications were made following this 1974 circuit.

Transistors Q3 and Q4 conduct alternately. The rate at which they switch is determined by the values of C1, C2, and the associated channel potentiometers connected to C3 and C4 through resistors R15 and R16. Were Q3 to conduct first when power was applied to the circuit, its collector voltage would be low; this would lower the voltage to the input of the counter circuit, IC1. The counter circuit is constructed in such a way that when its input voltage is low, it activates only one of the timing circuits connected to the base of Q4, which, when energized, charges capacitor C1 and causes the voltage at the base of Q4 to rise. When the base voltage reaches a high enough level, Q4 turns on and its collector voltage drops. This low voltage, coupled through C2 to the base of Q3, turns off Q3. Then Q3's collector voltage rises and the counter is triggered again through pin 5 of the IC and activates the next channel in the sequence. Transistor Q3 remains cut off until C2 charges to a level sufficient to allow Q3 to conduct again.

This action continues to the end of the 9th pulse when R17, which governs the input voltage to pin 8 of the IC, provides a longer charge time for C1 and, therefore, produces a sync pause of 5 msec.

Notice that pins 9 through 16 of IC1, with the exception of pin 13, are connected to 10K potentiometers. The potentiometers control the voltage applied to the timing channels through the movement of the control sticks, levers, and switches. The larger the voltage applied by the control, the less the associated servo will move; the smaller the voltage applied, the greater the servo movement.

Q1 and Q2 are used to quickly charge capacitors C1 and C2. This is necessary to prevent interaction between adjacent channels (keep them separated). If these capacitors were not completely charged, the conduction time of Q3 and Q4 would be shorter; the operation time of each channel would be shorter.

Diodes D4 through D10 prevent the negative voltage at the base of Q3 (or Q4) from discharging to ground during the time it is off.

Modulator transistors Q5 and Q6 form a monostable multivibrator that produces a 350 μsec off pulse each time Q3 or Q4 starts to conduct. As Q3 and Q4 conduct alternately, they produce pulses at their collectors that are coupled to D3 through C5. D3 allows only the negative half of each pulse to be coupled to the base of Q5, causing Q5 to conduct. A positive pulse from Q5 is coupled through C8 to the base of Q6. The duration of this pulse, also 350 μsec, is determined by C8 and R14. When Q6 is not conducting, its collector voltage is low. R12 provides positive DC feedback to the base of Q5 to keep it conducting when Q6 is not.

The RF and doubler circuits also receive their power from the collector of Q6. Thus, when the collector voltage of Q6 is low, the oscillator and buffer circuits are cut off; the pulse that arrives cuts off the signal in the same manner as described for the Kraft system (the transmitter is modulated by pulses whose width is varied). There is a slight difference between this and Kraft's system. In this system part of the output signal is taken from the antenna network and rectified by a diode to provide DC to operate a sensitive meter that indicates relative signal strength and RF output.

The forerunner of the modern control-pulse system is the pulse width/pulse spacing type (Fig. 5-10), which is still used today. The idea is to send out a single *on* pulse whose duration can be varied. This system has a special servo motor that is magnetically actuated; rather than moving gradually, it moves back and forth from one extreme position to another in time with pulse transmissions. Reduction gearing is not used in this kind of unit; a small crank affixed directly to the rotary (moving) part moves an airplane rudder back and forth and back again continuously. Although this system is simple in mechanical construction, it does produce a constant drain on the battery. A relay (electromechanical switch) operated by the receiver's output turns the battery voltage on and off in perfect time to the pulses' width and spacing. This system is best suited for rudder-control-only operation. With some modifications, however, motor control is possible (by changing the pulse repetition rate). For those who want to get into radio control as a hobby but are limited economically, this system will fill the bill. But there are slightly more than the average number of problems with this kind of system. You must make a test flight and then trim the airplane itself by adjusting its control surfaces. The Pulse Commander system shown can be useful for small airplanes being flown in confined areas. If you don't want to make a substantial initial investment, this is a good starter system; it can also serve as a second system, one for just "foolinaround" close to home,

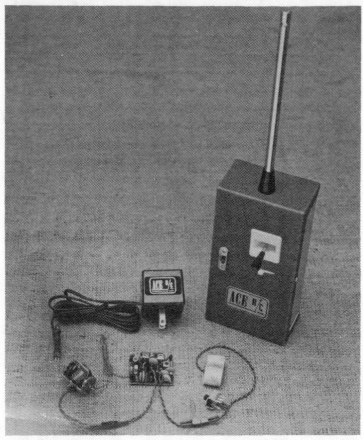

Fig. 5-10. The Ace Pulse Commander is a simple transmitter that allows only rudder control.

while another more elaborate one is reserved for more serious use: Sunday fly-ins and contests.

Assuming you're the average RC modeler, you're probably not licensed to make repairs or adjustments to your radio-control equipment if it gives you trouble. I recommend you return it to the manufacturer who is better equipped than anyone else to fix it. Most of the companies have nearby field representatives who can handle almost any situation adequately, from fixing broken PC boards to replacing malfunctioning transistors. But, before you send your gear in for repair—giving up a favorite avocation at the same time—make sure your battery is up to snuff and that all connectors are making complete contact; carbon tetrachloride, alcohol, or acetone, used with cotton swabs or small paint brushes, are excellent for cleaning contacts. Of course, you may have the facilities and knowledge to systematically troubleshoot a radio-control transmitter (although usually transmitter failure is due to poor transistor performance, and therefore is irreparable). If there is no RF output, check the voltage to the circuit board, inspect for hairline cracks in the printed-circuit board, and look for bad solder joints. Using a magnifying glass and continuity tester (or VOM), test each joint by pushing against it with an appropriate probe; reheat suspect joints, taking care not to let solder overflow. If your efforts in these areas prove fruitless, check the operation of the oscillator; the crystal may have to be changed if slight tuning of the coil doesn't remedy the situation.

If there is RF output but no pulse transmission, check the free-running multivibrator; an oscilloscope is necessary for verify the output of these transmitter stages. You may have to check the various one-shot multivibrators if just some pulses are missing; remember, if one fails, all that follow it will be inoperative. And don't overlook the antenna; loose sections or sections partially extended will cause erratic operation and a reduction in range.

If pulse-production seems okay, but the RF output is low, check your batteries after they have been connected to a load for several minutes. If the batteries are okay return the transmitter or try a replacement crystal.

Potentiometer wiper noise can be seen on an oscilloscope by moving a control stick with a spring centering device and releasing it; noise will appear as spikes in the normal waveform. Noisy potentiometers should be replaced to prevent erratic system operation.

RECEIVER TYPES

The operation of most modern receivers is about the same; the decoding methods used by various types may vary slightly but, basically, all operate on the same principles. The two fundamental types of receiver that are used for radio control are superregenerative and superheterodyne; under the latter category come single- and dual-conversion types.

Although superregenerative receivers (Fig. 5-11) have been quite popular in the past, the fact that they function by regenerating a signal and, therefore, emit their own radiation, has made their popularity decline for RC use; but they are suitable for operation in isolated areas or indoors. Also they are basically single-channel devices (offering only one control) that are not readily adaptable to proportional operation.

In spite of its drawbacks, the superregenerative receiver seems to satisfy the size requirement of very small aircraft; it can be built with a minimum of electronic components. And, by using tones for modulation, it is possible to obtain relatively interference-free superregenerative operation.

"Superhet" receivers are not only free of the radiation problems associated with superrengenerative types, their great stability and sensitivity make them the best choice for radio control. Superheterodyne receivers contain a *local oscillator*, whose output is mixed (by a *mixer*) with the incoming signal to produce frequencies representing the sum and difference of the two, which are *intermediate-frequency* or IF stage. A diagram of a local oscillator can be seen in the lower left corner of Fig. 5-12, a schematic for a superhet receiver; the IF stages are labeled IFT-1, -2, and -3.

DECODING

By turning the input tuning coil to the lower of the mixer's frequencies, 455 kHz, the higher is automatically rejected. The

Fig. 5-11. Superregenerative receivers must be tuned on frequency by turning a slug within a coil (lower left corner of PC board); this receiver will operate an escapement or Adams actuator directly.

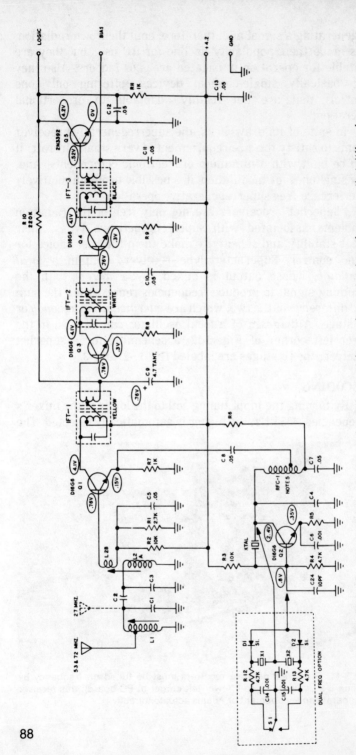

Fig. 5-12. Superheterodyne receiver schematic; crystals are chosen to give a frequency that differs from that of the incoming signal by the IF. (Component values dependent on operating band are not shown.) (Courtesy Heath Co.)

output of the IF stages is increased by a series of transistors, the last of which removes all traces of the RF signal, leaving the same kind of DC pulses generated by the transmitter. This transistor is often called a detector or second detector; the mixer stage is often called a first detector in a superhet receiver. The DC pulses are received by a decoder (schematic, Fig. 5-13).

In the decoder schematic, resistor R14 forward biases diode D3 to a voltage just below the forward-conduction point of the base/emitter junction of detector transistor Q5 (Fig. 5-12) and pulse amplifier Q6. Q5 is the output transistor of the receiver; the voltage developed across R14 turns on these two transistors.

R15 and R16 form a voltage-divider network that biases D4 to the point where only the top 0.6 or 0.7 volt of the spiked pulses coming from the receiver IFT amplifiers are transmitted to pulse amplifier Q6. Resistor R17 acts to unload the detector collector; C17 passes the pulse portion of the signal to the base of Q6. C18 filters out any oscillations at 455 kHz that might be present. R18 and R19 set the bias level for Q6.

With a low signal or no signal, the voltage at pin 5 of IC1 is high. The output at pin 6 is therefore low, so register IC2 is cleared, and all outputs will be low. This is true even though the clock (multivibrator) pulses and serial (control) pulses are high at pins 1 and 2 of IC2. The clock pulse is the sync pulse. So there is no output from the register under this condition. When the signal input increases, D5 conducts. This discharges C20, causing the clear line to go to a high voltage. This *enables* the register; the register will now produce an output when it has an input at pins 1 and 2. The reason for the low-signal condition mentioned earlier is so the control system will not operate unless there is a strong enough signal to insure reliable operation. It also insures that all outputs are low when the transmitter is off; this prevents servos from moving controls to maximum deflection in the absence of a command.

C21, a sync detector, is kept discharged by the pulse frame, but in the absence of pulses (during the sync pause), it will charge through the gate resistance of IC2. When the voltage across C21 reaches 1.2 volts, it *arms* the register: it has the voltage necessary for its operation; the first pulse following the sync pause will cause the channel one output

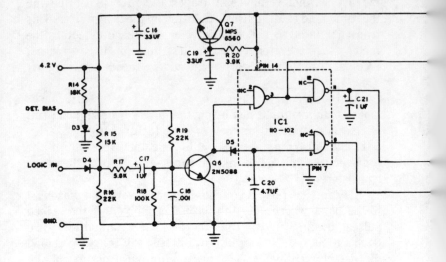

(from register pin 3) to be a temporarily high voltage. The second pulse will do the same for channel two, and so on. As each channel goes to a high-voltage output, the preceding channel drops back again to a low-level output. Thus the decoder causes voltage to be applied to each channel in exact response to transmitted pulses (that exist for the duration of control pulses). It also causes the channeling of the pulses to individual channels.

So far only single-conversion receivers have been described, that is, those with one local oscillator. Dual-conversion rigs use two (Fig. 5-14). The incoming signal is mixed with the output of a first oscillator, and the difference signal, at a high intermediate frequency, is mixed with output of a second oscillator for a second IF. This kind of operation reduces losses that result from converting very high frequencies —144, 220, or 465 MHz—directly to 455 kHz. Instead the signal is first reduced to 10 MHz, which is converted to 455 kHz in the second mixing operation. The benefits of this are greater selectivity and sensitivity.

RECEIVER PERFORMANCE

Selectivity is the measure of a receiver's ability to reject unwanted signals. Figure 5-15 gives a graphic comparison of characteristics for receivers with broad or poor selectivity,

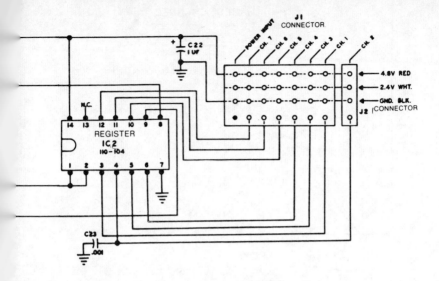

Fig. 5-13. Receiver decoder schematic. (Courtesy Heath Co.)

and good or narrow selectivity. Reception can be broad if the receiver doesn't have enough IF stages. But it can be too selective. Radio-control receivers must have enough bandwidth (nonselectivity) to pass transmitted pulses without distortion. The narrower the pulses, the wider the bandpass response required. In some equipment ceramic filters rather

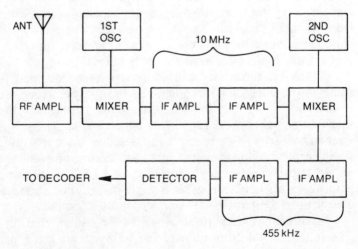

Fig. 5-14. Block diagram of a dual-conversion superheterodyne receiver.

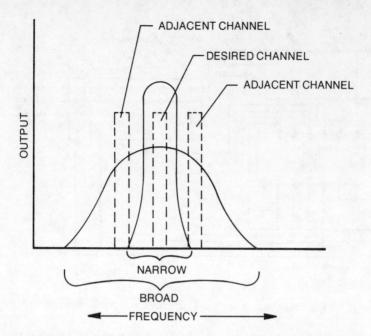

Fig. 5-15. A comparison of selectivity curves; a narrow, flat-topped curve is ideal.

than IF stages are used; they never need tuning or adjusting. Ceramic filters, about the size of transistors, will only pass the frequency to which they are resonant (the difference signal of a superhet receiver). Much like a bell being struck by its clapper, a crystal filter resonates or produces an output when fed a signal in tune with its natural (resonant) frequency and no other. Because they don't require tuning and don't use coils, they are much more desirable than slug-tuned IF stages.

Combined, selectivity and sensitivity make for what is commonly termed good reception. The sensitivity of a receiver is determined by the lowest input signal needed for the specified signal-to-noise ratio of its output signal. There is a limit on how sensitive a receiver can be made. If too sensitive, it will respond to the arcing of cars' distributors, or even pick up electrical interference from some of its fellow airborne passengers, its neighboring servos; yet it should be sensitive enough to be compatible with your transmitter's output.

Sensitivity is important when you consider that the transmitted signal drops off, as received, by an amount equal to the inverse of the range squared:

$$signal = \frac{1}{range^2}$$

So you can see that it doesn't take much of an increase in range to cause a big reduction in the signal seen by the receiver.

Fortunately, superhet RC receivers incorporate an automatic gain control (AGC), a circuit that takes some of the receiver's output and returns it as an input; this keeps the output at a nearly constant level. This means that although your airplane is flying directly away from you (and the transmitter) and the signal it receives is getting weaker, the AGC is "turning up the volume." It also "reduces the volume" as the airplane comes back for a landing. In this manner, control remains constant and smooth, regardless of where the plane happens to be.

For best performance, a superregenerative receiver should be tuned with its antenna placed in its final position on the plane. When tuning this type of receiver, try to keep as far from the antenna as possible to minimize the capacitive effects between it and your body.

Superhet receivers are usually factory-tuned, but their antennas must be kept clear of anything metal when they are installed aboard a plane; the antenna should not be mounted or run near metal pushrods, or even near metallic paint. The best way to route the antenna is out of the cabin and back to the vertical stabilizer as directly as possible.

6

Servos

The requirements for a model radio-control servo are that it be light, strong, and use little electricity. It must be reversible in motion, from forward or clockwise to reverse or counterclockwise, by simply reversing the battery connections to it (in practice, accomplished by two transistors in a motor-control circuit). It must be reliable enough to keep from binding when stopped during its rotation, and rugged enough to withstand extreme temperatures and the vibration encountered in airplanes.

The servo motors used today, a type first developed in Japan for camera equipment and later adapted to RC use, are very small units (Fig. 6-1). Although servo motors are commonly electric, in some systems they can be pneumatic, hydraulic, or spring-driven; so it is best, for clearest communication, to say *electric* servo motor when that's what is meant.

A servo amplifier is a unit that supplies sufficient (and controlled) power to make a servo motor run. This unit takes, as an input, a very tiny signal from the receiver decoder and amplifies it for its output, which is released in precisely controlled, larger values of electric current for the motor's operation. It also governs the direction of the motor's rotation in response to the kind of input signal it receives; in our systems, pulse width governs the direction of rotation.

Fig. 6-1. This RC servo motor exemplifies the miniaturization techniques used today.

Any pulse narrower than the pulse transmitted when controls are in their neutral position will make the motor run in one direction, while those that are wider cause it to go in the opposite direction; the amount of motor movement is a function of how much wider or narrower the pulses are compared to a neutral pulse.

A steady reference pulse is generated by the servo amplifier in the absence of a transmitted control pulse. But when the motor is directed to move, it also moves a potentiometer connected to its output shaft that matches the width of the reference pulse.

Using plastic gearing, the servo moves a control arm that is connected by a rigid or flexible linkage (pushrod) to a rudder, elevator, motor throttle, etc. Proportional control makes the system keep itself in balance by matching its pulses to control pulses. Besides being limited in its movement by transmitted control pulses, servo motors can also incorporate stops or limit switches.

The servomechanism (from which *servo* is derived) is usually an enclosed unit containing control circuits, a motor, gears, and a feedback potentiometer (Fig. 6-2). In the photo the black arms are connected to the servo output shaft, and the white arms are linkages used to redirect the motion of the output arms. Servos can also be employed individually, one for each control channel (Fig. 6-3).

Fig. 6-2. Servo packages can be easily mounted within model aircraft; the additional linkage (disconnected) gives greater versitility in pushrod movement.

PROPORTIONAL CONTROL

The power for servo operation comes from a servo amplifier that takes as an input a very tiny signal from the receiver decoder and amplifies it for its output, which is released in precisely controlled, larger values of electric current to run the motor. A steady reference pulse is generated by the servo amplifier in the absence of a transmitted control pulse. But when the motor is directed to move, it also moves a potentiometer connected to its output

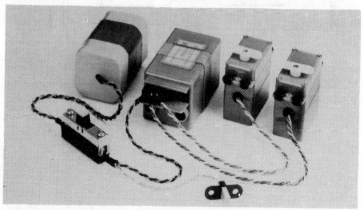

Fig. 6-3. Servos can be used individually, one for each control channel; those shown give rudder and motor control. (Courtesy EK Products, Inc.)

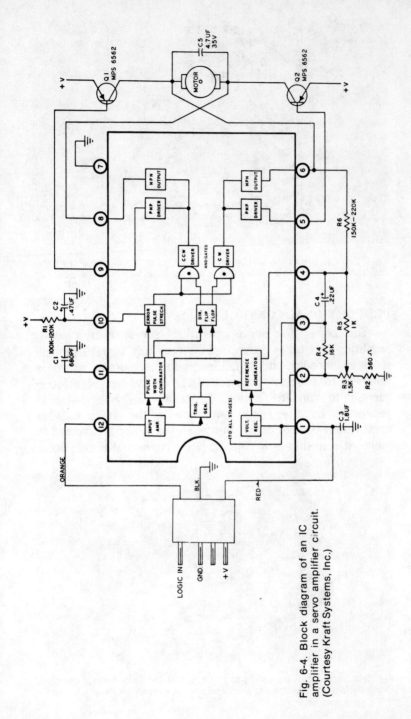

Fig. 6-4. Block diagram of an IC amplifier in a servo amplifier circuit. (Courtesy Kraft Systems, Inc.)

98

shaft that matches the width of the reference pulse to that of the control pulse. When the pulses are matched, the motor shuts off—thus this method of RC operation gives proportional control, the motor starting and stopping when commanded to do so. Any pulse narrower than the pulse transmitted when controls are in their neutral position will make the motor run in one direction, while those that are wider cause it to go in the opposite direction; the amount of motor movement is a function of how much wider or narrower the pulses are compared to a neutral control pulse.

CIRCUIT OPERATION

The development of the integrated circuit has done much for the reliability and compactness of servos. The IC servo amplifier shown in the block diagram Fig. 6-4, is a Schmitt-trigger type. It is completely integrated except for timing components and output transistors. The IC features a temperature-compensated voltage regulator for reference-pulse generator power and provides stable operation from −25°C to 75°C, using 2.8 to 6.0 volts (supply). A special feature is the use of a single "pulse-stretching" capacitor that provides equal, minimum pulse-width drive in both error directions. The output transistors are outside the package but within the servo case (on the amplifier chassis) to minimize voltage drops and keep heat dissipation low.

The input pulse at pin 12 is amplified and applied to one side of the pulse-width comparator. The trigger generator drives a pulse suitable for initiating the one-shot multivibrator from the leading edge of the input pulse. The reference-pulse generator is powered by an internal voltage regulator that makes the one-shot multivibrator nearly immune to transient voltages; the supply is temperature compensated so that it maintains nearly zero drift over its entire operating range. The resistors and capacitors connected to pins 2 through 4 control reference generator pulse width.

R3, a potentiometer (Fig. 6-5), is moved by the servo motor to reestablish pulse matching when an input pulse is received; this is the feedback potentiometer. R6, a damping resistor, causes the servo motor to stop running as soon as its voltage is removed. (Normally such a motor would coast and overshoot its desired arm position.) R6 also prevents overshooting when the servo motor makes large movements

Fig. 6-5. A wiper assembly (left) and resistive element (center) make up the feedback potentiometer.

as commanded by large changes in control-pulse width. The output of the reference generator is connected to one side of the pulse-width comparator. This circuit, after comparing the widths of incoming and reference pulses, supplies an output pulse to both the error-pulse stretcher and the proper side of the direction-controlling flip-flop; it does this whenever there is any difference between the width of input pulses and the reference pulses' width.

In servo systems like this, it is impossible to adjust the reference pulse to exactly cancel the input pulse. There will always be a tiny residual voltage when they are as closely nulled (balanced) as possible. This tolerance, which allows some alteration of the error pulse without affecting the input to the servo motor, is called the *dead band*; capacitor C1 is used to slow comparator operation so proper adjustment of the servo dead band can be made.

If the dead band remaining at the null position is large, the servo motor has not exactly reached the position it was supposed to; so the rudder, elevator, or other control surface it is connected to will not be in the required position: precise airplane control will be lost. On the other hand, if the circuits are adjusted so that the null is too critical, the dead band will become so small that the servo motor's momentum will cause it to overshoot its desired position (in spite of the damping resistor) and its arm will "hunt" or vibrate around every position it is commanded to. Hunting is bad because it uses up battery power needlessly. (Increasing the value of C1 widens the dead band.)

The error-pulse stretcher lengthens the error pulse (whose width is the difference between the command pulse and the reference pulse) enough to make the motor run whenever the width of the dead band is exceeded. The minimum pulse width is normally 3 msec; anything less than that is insufficient for servo motor operation in this particular system (other systems may have different requirements). The pulse stretcher's polarity will be the same regardless of the error pulse's *direction*: command pulse wider than reference pulse or reference pulse wider than command pulse. The direction is determined by a flip-flop, which changes state only when the error pulse becomes wider or narrower than normal. The outputs of the flip-flop are fed to two AND gates (amplifiers) that turn on the appropriate driver transistors. The AND gates also receive an input from the error-pulse stretcher; both inputs must be present for an output from the AND gates.

The two direction drivers apply the current necessary for the output transistors located on the IC board, and for the driver stage, which supplies base current to the external output transistors.

SERVO BREAKDOWN

Most of the severe problems associated with servos are brought about by damaged solid-state devices on the amplifier board (Fig. 6-6). A defective output transistor can cause the servo to rotate in only one direction; an IC that is defective

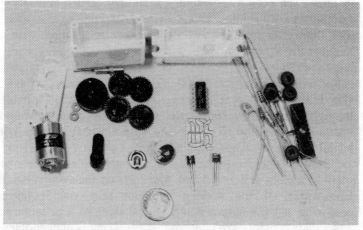

Fig. 6-6. Servo kit. The IC amplifier and its printed-circuit board are shown in the center of the photo.

could cause a lack of output for motion in either direction. These are not user-serviceable parts and must be replaced.

Servo troubles may be caused by a faulty feedback potentiometer or a defective motor. If a servo control arm vibrates or jumps around when being positioned, the problem can usually be traced to the feedback potentiometer; if cleaning it doesn't remedy the problem, it has to be replaced. A malfunctioning servo motor can be responsible for controls hanging up before reaching their desired deflection, slow servo arm movement, or for complications resulting from noise it generates. Fortunately, less severe problems can usually be attributed to poor battery performance (see the following chapter for maintenance tips).

SERVO SERVICING

The exploded view of a servo shown in Fig. 6-7 should demonstrate how vulnerable this mechanism is to fouling caused by dirt. With some care, a jeweler's screwdriver, solvent, and lubricant, a servo can be kept in tip-top shape. Assuming yours is like the servo shown in the drawing and you suspect that long use and exposure to dirt indicates a cleaning, begin by removing the output arms and wheel. Next remove the screws or tape holding the case top and gently take it off, being very careful not to upset the gear train. Firmly establish in your mind how the gear train is assembled before you take it apart—it may help to make a rough sketch of the layout and identify each gear by scratching a number on it representing its place in the assembly order. After disassembling the gears, soak them in a small pan of alcohol, then scrub them with a toothbrush. When you are sure they are clean, carefully inspect each for chipped, bent, or broken teeth (a magnifying glass would be helpful for this). The most commonly damaged gear is the output gear (shown); replacements are available through most hobby shops. Reassemble the gear train and install the case top. Replace the output wheel—but do not install its screw; an operational checkout should be made first.

Plug the servo into the aileron channel (assuming four or more channels are available) and turn on the receiver and transmitter. If the servo's behavior tells you it needs centering, set the output wheel on the shaft so it is centered when your controls are centered. If centering is unnecessary, then control the servo throughout its entire range of movement; it should be smooth in operation in both directions. If you are satisfied with its performance, put the screws in the top cover, fasten on the output wheel and arms, and make sure the assembly is secure. Now check for neutral positioning. Does the servo return to the neutral position everytime the controls are in neutral? Or does your servo jitter or creep; these symptoms usually point to a dirty feedback potentiometer.

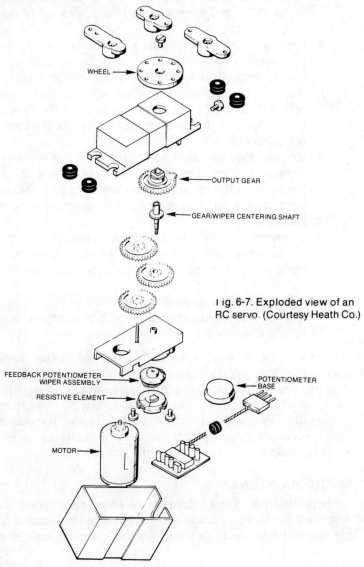

WHEEL

OUTPUT GEAR

GEAR/WIPER CENTERING SHAFT

Fig. 6-7. Exploded view of an RC servo. (Courtesy Heath Co.)

FEEDBACK POTENTIOMETER WIPER ASSEMBLY

POTENTIOMETER BASE

RESISTIVE ELEMENT

MOTOR

CURING "THE JITTERS"

Basically, "the jitters" or creeping is caused by copper residue buildup on the wiper arm that prevents it from seating against the resistive element properly; and so the arm hunts for a place where it can make contact and stop. This leads to fluctuating reference pulses. The solution, in this case, is to clean and lubricate the potentiometer elements:

- Remove the output wheel and case bottom (referring to Fig. 6-7); you may have to take screws out of the case top to do this.
- Carefully lift out the printed-circuit board, noting its placement, connections to it, and how its leads are routed within the case. You should now be able to see the base of the feedback potentiometer. (For some servos it may not be necessary to take out the circuit board; opening the case top may expose the feedback potentiometer.)
- Remove the two small screws securing the resistive element to the potentiometer assembly and note its positioning; the alignment notches in its edge, being equal in size and spacing, cannot be used as guides to reassembly.
- Clean the contact side of the wiper assembly and the resistive element with alcohol or contact cleaner, using a cotton swab; also inspect the wiper for any distortion.
- Apply a small amount of petroleum jelly on the face side of the resistive element with a toothpick and spread it evenly for a thin film; reassemble the servo.

This would be a good time to center the output arm electrically. Turn on the receiver and plug the servo into it. With its trim controls centered, turn on the transmitter. If the servo output arm does not center, use a jeweler's screwdriver to turn the centering shaft (shown) located under the output arm's screw slightly in the direction of centering error; continue making adjustments until the arm centers.

MOTOR MAINTENANCE

Servicing the motor requires the same disassembly as described for servo cleaning but extending to the removal of the motor. Before undoing the motor itself, scratch matching

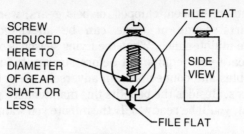

SCREW REDUCED HERE TO DIAMETER OF GEAR SHAFT OR LESS

FILE FLAT

SIDE VIEW

FILE FLAT

Fig. 6-8. A gear puller is slipped under the gear from the side, then the screw is turned against the gear shaft, disengaging the gear.

marks on the motor plate and case, so they can be aligned properly later; misalignment will affect the relationship of magnets to brushes, thus affecting motor performance. Use a gear puller (Fig. 6-8) to remove the motor shaft gear. Take off the motor plate and armature, being careful to keep track of any washers. Spread the brushes and remove the armature from the motor plate. Clean the commutator with alcohol and polish it with as fine an abrasive paper as you can find; blueprint paper would do, but the carbonless-copy paper used to duplicate charge-card receipts is probably handier. Clean the brushes curved surfaces with a very fine round or half-round file. The servo's reassembly follows a check of the wire connections to the brush posts. The easiest way to test the motor is with a servo controller (Fig. 6-9); lacking this, you will have to interconnect the servo and receiver and use your transmitter.

Notice that the problems affecting servo operation fall into three general categories: worn or dirty feedback

Fig. 6-9. Using this device, a servo can be run through its paces without having to be plugged into an activated receiver.

potentiometer; broken, chipped, or bent gears; worn or dirty motor parts. Some of these can be alleviated through preventive maintenance. When the flying season is over, clean and lubricate your equipment before storing it; fuel residue left on cables and connectors can adversely affect them over long periods. Besides the benefits this maintenance gives your equipment, you'll be ready to fly the minute you want to.

7

Batteries for the RC Equipment

Until recently, dry cells were without gears for powering RC equipment, but their reliability often had to be insured by making up several battery packs that were replaced as frequently as every other flight. Today this kind of cell can almost be considered an oddity for any application. Its rival for RC use is the rechargeable nickel-cadmium battery or *nicad*.

INSIDE THE NICAD

A nicad battery (Fig. 7-1) is a package of cells, just as an automobile battery is a package of cells (six 2-volt cells in a 12-volt battery, for example). Where a car battery uses lead electrodes and a sulphuric-acid electrolyte, the nicad contains nickel- and cadmium-based elements working in a jellied potassium-hydroxide electrolyte. Instead of plates, the electrodes are actually alternating layers of powered metal pressed or sintered onto a backing and furled into a "jelly roll" (Fig. 7-2).

Each battery typically contains four cells rated at 1.2 volts for a total voltage of 4.8 volts; one such "pack" would power a receiver, while two would be needed for a transmitter (Fig. 7-3).

CHARGE CAPACITY

It is a characteristic of nicad packs that they will very slowly discharge to 4.4 volts and then continue to discharge

Fig. 7-1. Transmitter nicad pack; care must be taken not to spring the male terminal connector. (Courtesy Kraft Systems, Inc.)

quite rapidly thereafter (Fig. 7-4) to a voltage unusable by the equipment being powered. For the RC modeler this can mean sudden loss of plane control. Because a nicad can lose its charge so fast beyond its initially slow discharge rate, and therefore be responsible for a downed plane, it is important that it not only be kept charged, it must also be kept at its maximum capacity for retaining a charge. Figure 7-5 illustrates how a nicad left in storage loses this capacity over time. The process used to help a nicad keep its charging capacity is *cycling*: the battery is discharged to about 4.4 volts (never below 1.1 volts per cell), then charged fully over a period of 14 to 16 hours. (It is unfortunate that the equipment normally used to do this can't duplicate the sudden current demands of operating servos as a check of the battery's ability to perform under actual flight conditions.) The charging rate for a nicad pack is closely related to its capacity for delivering a specified current over a given time period; this is stated in milliampere-hours or mAh (however, a 500 mAh battery will not provide 500 mA for 1 hour—its actually 50 mA for 10 hours).

BATTERY LIFE

If the airplane's design allows the increase in payload, battery drain can be halved by using two batteries connected *in parallel*: positive terminals are interconnected, as are negative terminals, then either of each pair is connected to the equipment needing power (Fig. 7-6) for double the charge life.

The cells within batteries are connected *in series*: electrically connected the way cells are seen to be connected in flashlights; so in packs that are connected in parallel, the *cells* are connected in *series-parallel*.

All this is not to say that RC equipment manufacturers undersupply their products electrically; it's just a way (where feasible) to defeat the RC modeler's prime nemesis, battery failure. Fortunately, there are a few companies looking out for the model flyer's interests in this area too. Battery condition monitors are available that indicate remaining battery voltage using LEDS (light-emitting diodes—similar to those used in

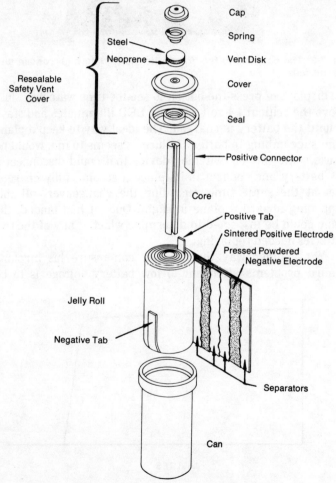

Fig. 7-2. Exploded view of a Union Carbide nicad cell.

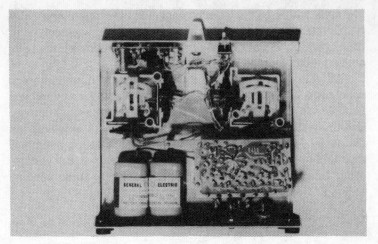

Fig. 7-3. The batteries in this transmitter (lower left) both contain four 1.2-volt cells.

the displays of press-the-button-to-see-the-time watches). Just above the critical 4.4-volt level, an LED illuminates and stays lit until the battery is charged. The ideal way to keep a plane from succumbing to battery failure, it seems to me, would be to use some sort of switching device that could disconnect a low battery and connect in its place a second, fully charged one—at the same time recording the changeover—all this happening aboard a plane in flight. Once it had landed, the plane could be inspected to determine which if any of the two batteries needed replacing.

Yet another way the modeler can insure his airplane against problems attendant to low battery voltage is to be

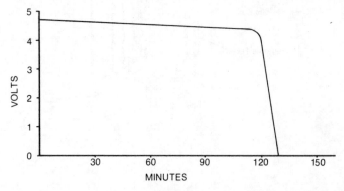

Fig. 7-4. Discharge curve for a 4.8-volt nicad pack in use.

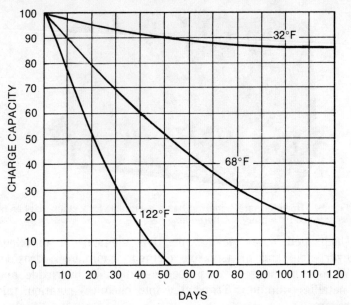

Fig. 7-5. The graph shows the loss of a nicad's capacity to retain a charge at sample temperatures; stored at 68°F, a nicad will be down to 70% of its charge capacity in a month.

aware of any aberrant behavior it exhibits in flight and luggish or erratic control-surface movements during its preflight tests.

VOLTAGE RESTORATION

The purpose of charging a battery is to restore its voltage by reversing the internal chemical process that creates it.

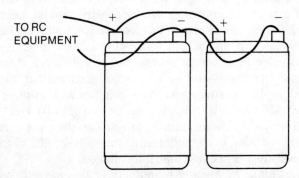

Fig. 7-6. Nicad packs can be connected in parallel to maximize their charge life; either terminal in an interconnected pair can be used as a connection point.

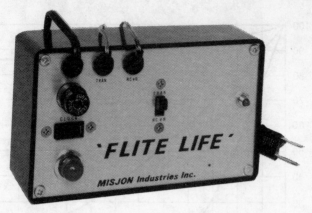

Fig. 7-7. This charger/discharger has a receptacle for a clock that can be used to record battery discharge time.

Uncharged, the nicad's positive element is nickelous hydroxide, and its negative element, cadmium hydroxide. When it's charged, these become nickelic hydroxide and metallic cadmium. Translated into chemical notation, this becomes

$$\text{(charged)} \longleftarrow \text{(discharged)}$$
$$Cd + Ni(OH)_3 \longrightarrow Cd(OH)_2 + Ni(OH)_2$$

The opposing arrows indicate that the process is reversible. During the latter part of a charging cycle, nickel-cadmium batteries generate gas: oxygen at the positive electrode, hydrogen at the negative electrode. These gases must be vented from the battery. However, in order to have a cell that can be charged and sealed (as in RC battery packs), the accumulation of hydrogen must be prevented. One battery manufacturer accomplishes this by constructing its nicads so that when they are charged, the positive electrode reaches its full charge first and starts generating oxygen. Because the negative electrode has not yet reached its full charge, it cannot generate hydrogen; the cells are designed so that oxygen formed at the positive electrode reaches and oxidizes the negative electrode. During overcharge, the negative electrode is oxidized at a rate just sufficient to offset the input energy; the cell remains in "equilibrium" indefinitely, the negative electrode always just less than fully charged.

Cells made by another manufacturer become self-venting while they gas, resealing themselves when charging is discontinued.

112

CHARGER/DISCHARGERS

Unlike the units that accompany rechargeable shavers and other small appliances that can be electrically rejuvenated, the operation of some RC nicad chargers includes a discharge cycle and, hence, are called charger/dischargers. The Flite Life Rite charger/discharger (Fig. 7-7), being representative of the latest developments in this area, includes a receptacle that takes the electrical plug of an ordinary clock, which is used to keep track of the battery's discharge rate, an indication of its capacity to retain a charge. The clock is set to 12 o'clock and plugged into the unit, and the discharge cycle is initiated. When the critical voltage value is reached (4.4) the unit shuts off automatically and the clock stops, leaving a record of the discharge time. There is also a light that stays on while the battery voltage remains above 4.4 volts for a receiver pack or 9.2 volts for the two packs required in a transmitter.

On a more elaborate scale, another version of this type of equipment offers two built-in timers (Fig. 7-8). Its operation can accommodate nicad packs for a receiver and transmitter and gives simultaneous charge/discharge functions—features that get you ready for the flying field in short order. At the other end of the scale is the simpler, more compact variety of chargers; to the right of the 110-volt unit shown in Fig. 7-9 is a

Fig. 7-8. Built-in timers in this charger/discharger record the discharge time for two sets of batteries simultaneously.

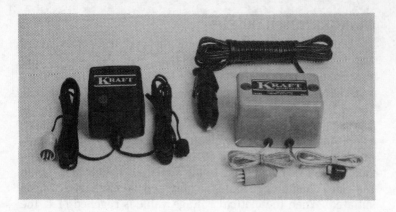

Fig. 7-9. The isolation transformers in these chargers, one made to plug into a wall outlet (left) and the other adaptable to a car cigarette lighter, prevent the hazard of shock.

charger that can be used in a car (note the cigarette lighter plug).

There are other methods of verifying battery condition using similar equipment in conjunction with an expanded-scale voltmeter. One manufacturer offers a voltmeter that plugs into the charging receptacle of its receiver pack; if the meter indicates more than 4.4 volts (at a 250 mA drain current) for at least 2 hours, the pack can be considered safe to fly with.

Although most complete RC systems include a charger/discharger, some modelers who also dabble in building electronic gear devise their own. Figure 7-10 is a schematic for such a homebrew device submitted by one of my RC hobbyist/correspondents. Any transformer capable of supplying the power necessary for the charging circuit can be used. A bridge rectifier is used with a capacitive filter for the DC supply. Zener voltages are determined by setting R8, R9, and R10 (potentiometers). Any of three resistors, R1 through R3, can be switched into the circuit depending on the discharge rate desired. The voltage developed across the resistor selected is compared to the voltage set by resistors R8 through R10. When they are equal, the output of operational amplifier IC 741 goes to zero and the relay unlatches, disconnecting the discharge circuit, connecting the battery to the charge circuit, and stopping the clock in the power supply. Closing S4 momentarily initiates the discharge cycle. R11 is used to

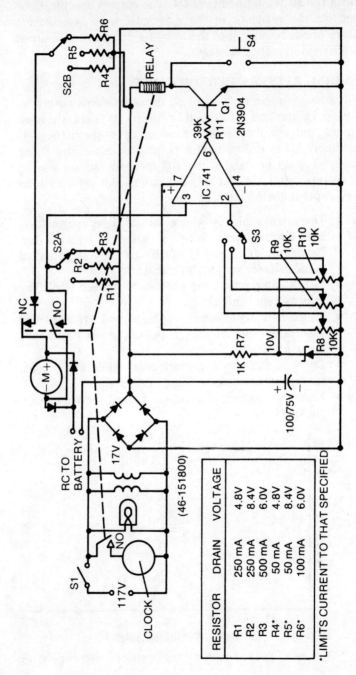

Fig. 7-10. Nicad charger/discharger schematic.

RESISTOR	DRAIN	VOLTAGE
R1	250 mA	4.8V
R2	250 mA	8.4V
R3	500 mA	6.0V
R4*	50 mA	4.8V
R5*	50 mA	8.4V
R6*	100 mA	6.0V

*LIMITS CURRENT TO THAT SPECIFIED

control the switching points of Q1. The current specifications given for the resistors in the schematic were selected for battery packs belonging to the circuit's designer; values can be chosen to fit individual needs.

INSURING BATTERY PERFORMANCE

It's really ironic that out of all the components aboard an RC model plane and those used to control its flight, the least complex, and one that uses no moving parts—the battery—is most likely to be responsible for putting a damper on a flying session. Try as he might, the RC modeler has no way of guaranteeing failsafe battery operation. But he can take measures that could save his plane:

- Don't leave nicads where they will be subjected to high temperatures (within a closed car on a hot day, for example); Fig. 7-11 illustrates the voltage loss of nicad cells for various temperatures.
- Check interconnecting cables for breaks (including intermittent conduction).
- Clean all connectors (plugs and receptacles) associated with voltage supplies, and see that they make a tight fit.
- Check a battery's performance while it is being subjected to simulated flight vibration.
- Make sure airborne batteries are well bedded in foam packing.

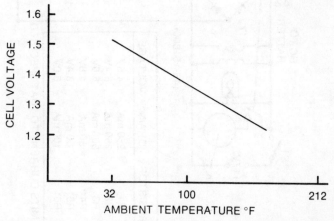

Fig. 7-11. A nicad cell's voltage will drop with increased ambient temperature.

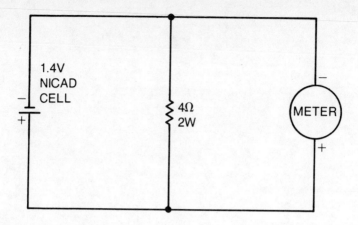

Fig. 7-12. Voltmeter/resistor arrangement for testing an individual nicad cell.

- Always check a new nicad pack before using it.
- Charge batteries no longer than a day before they are to be used.
- Put batteries in plastic bags where fuel-proofing is necessary.
- Make periodic checks on the condition of individual cells.

The last procedure recommended, carried out with a recently charged pack, requires a voltmeter and a 2-watt 4-ohm resistor connected to the cell as shown in Fig. 7-12. The meter should show at least 1.1 volts for 2 hours; if it doesn't, cycle the battery and repeat the test. Failure during the second test indicates a cell due for retirement (you can expect a nicad to see you through 300 to 600 cyclings).

8

Building an RC System

In a previous chapter it was pointed out that, advantages weighed against disadvantages, building a radio-control system from scratch is no real benefit to the aircraft modeler. The best way to go nowadays is to get a good kit. True to my own advice, that's exactly what I did to get back into the hobby; it had been 10 years since I had controlled a model plane in the air.

You do not have to be able to read schematics or have any experience in electronics to assemble a thoughtfully designed RC kit. In fact, a lack of experience could be to your advantage. Familiarity, it is said, breeds contempt; that phrase is certainly applicable to building kits, because it seems that some people, out of their "familiarity" with electronics gear, are contemptuous of instructions—they assemble things out of order, disregard cautions, put chassis screws in the wrong way. In the main, kit failures cannot be blamed on missing or damaged parts, unclear instructions, or poor design but on builder failure, failure to follow instructions.

The primary requisites for a kit under consideration are a complete complement of parts; clear, well-illustrated instructions; and a minimum tool requirement for making the rig work. With these criteria foremost in my mind, I made my selection. Of course, past experience has its influence; falling

Fig. 8-1. The transmitter shown in the foreground of this photo, a Heathkit model GD-1205-D, was the one chosen for the construction project; the model at the rear has a control stick that can be rotated (note the knob) for rudder or aileron control.

back on a brand used in days gone by, I chose a Heath system, specifically, an eight-channel dual-stick model (transmitter shown in foreground of Fig. 8-1) operable on any of the three RC bands; this represents just about the ultimate in control flexibility. What I learned from its assembly is the essence of this chapter.

Included with the kit is a direct factory telephone number and the name of a representative to ask for if you have trouble or questions, although the written directions are clear enough—if you don't hurry, and read them carefully to be certain you understand what is said.

The completed receiver for the system is modular (Fig. 8-2) and has plug-in RF sections that allow changing bands easily; Fig. 8-3 demonstrates just how easily this can be done.

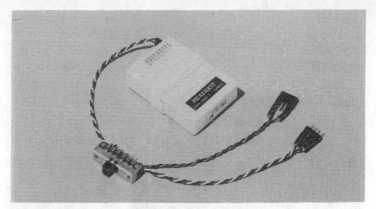

Fig. 8-2. All connections to this receiver are made quite easily through the use of connectors; the wire wrapped around it is its antenna.

RECEIVER ASSEMBLY

Although the plan of construction called for building the transmitter first, I was unable to do this because there was some delay in obtaining the parts for the first production run of this kit—and I was anxious to move ahead with this book. So I started with the receiver, even though I knew I would have to wait until the transmitter was constructed before I could test it. The usual procedure is to assemble the transmitter first, test it with a meter (supplied), and then use the transmitter and meter to test the receiver; the receiver and transmitter are later used together to test and adjust the servos. (So there

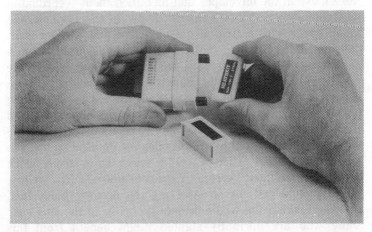

Fig. 8-3. Changing channels or bands is this easy: change modules.

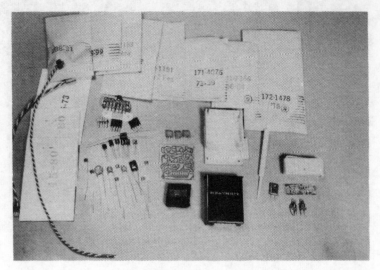

Fig. 8-4. Receiver parts array.

is good reason for the recommended sequence of construction steps.)

Unpacking the receiver parts boxes (Fig. 8-4) was reminiscent of undoing packages on Christmas day. The envelopes contain all the resistors, diodes, and other circuit components required; the instruction manual (not shown) came in the same package.

I chose the next step because of previous experience (it was not prohibited by the instructions). I took all the parts that were loose in the envelopes and identified them according to what they were and their values by fastening them to a piece of tablet paper with a strip of masking tape and labeling them appropriately (Fig. 8-5). Suffering—but not severely—from a slight case of color blindness, I was especially careful with the resistors; I have a little difficulty distinguishing certain shades of red and green and that made me wary of depending on resistor value bands. So I obtained an ohmmeter and measured each resistor; since there were many with the same value, I grouped them into little piles before affixing them to the tablet paper. Then I could select from them when necessary, without error. Time-consuming? Not really, because it helped me in selecting the proper values fast, thereby making the whole project go faster in the long run; some who are normally sighted might benefit from this method too.

The value of capacitors and other parts are easily discernible, but I segregated them according to my usual practice (as I had done with the resistors). I further categorized them by type, such as Mylar and ceramic.

If there's any ability besides literacy needed to build a kit, it's an ability to solder well. Adequate instructions on soldering are given with the kit and following them will insure success—if you get the recommended size of soldering iron and practice a bit before beginning on the kit. You should also watch an iron's tip as you use it to be sure it isn't pitting; this condition will reduce the heat available to the joint. In addition to constant wiping and tinning (putting a shiney solder coat on the tip), I used a file every now and then to keep a flat, chisel edge to the tip; this is particularly important when using small, low-powered irons.

Even though the manufacturer didn't recommend it, I kept a constant check on the top side of the chassis to make sure parts weren't mounted crookedly, permitting their wires to touch one another. Using a magnifying glass, I made certain nothing would be shorted through this kind of error. The need for inspecting the bottom of the chassis often for shorts across the circuit board is a matter of course; the procedure for this was given.

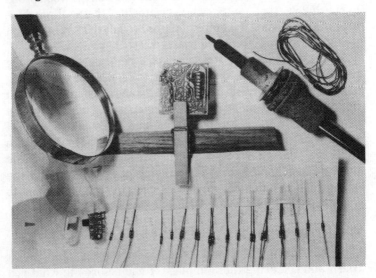

Fig. 8-5. The first printed-circuit board awaiting its components; the clothespin serves as a vise.

Fig. 8-6. View of receiver circuit board showing crystal filters (row of blocklike components across the top).

When building a kit, use care, take your time, and inspect everything often to be sure that you have the parts in the right holes before you solder them; that all solder joints are good (shiney) and the parts secure (you can use a small wood probe to push on the joints while watching them through a magnifying glass); that circuit paths are not shorted; and that parts are isolated from the chassis where they should be.

Working with tiny parts in confined spaces over long periods leads to, well, flakiness; this is conductive to selecting the wrong parts or positioning the right ones incorrectly. If you find yourself getting anxious about completing a kit, if you're tired, if your mind is really on something else—take a break. I found that hard concentration spent over 30- to 45-minute stretches was all I could afford to insure a good job. The break-taking approach to kit building pays dividends in the long run; it is much easier to do it right the first time than to make repairs later.

THE RF MODULE

After placing the parts on the receiver printed-circuit board and soldering them in place, I had before me what you see in Fig. 8-6. Figure 8-7 shows the completed circuit in its labeled case.

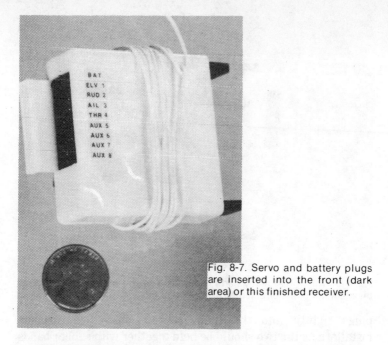

Fig. 8-7. Servo and battery plugs are inserted into the front (dark area) or this finished receiver.

The next step was constructing the RF module that is plugged into the receiver to establish its band of operation. Two were furnished with the kit, but others are obtainable for operation on any RC band from the manufacturer. (Be sure to get matching modules for the transmitter.) The crystal that governs the frequency of the RF module can be seen at the bottom of the circuit board in Fig. 8-8. Although the RF module

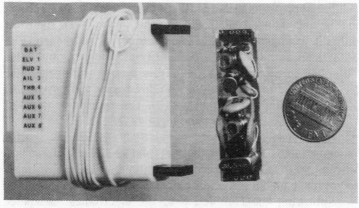

Fig. 8-8. The RF module (center) without its case.

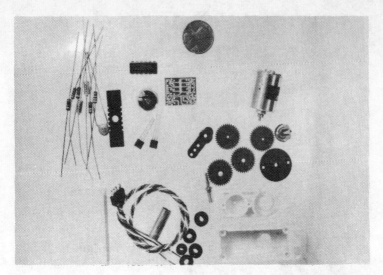

Fig. 8-9. Not all that many parts comprise a servo—but notice how close the diameter of the circuit board is to that of the penny.

plugs tightly into the main receiver body, in airplane installations the two should be held together with rubber bands to prevent their possible separation in flight. The receiver is not designed to be mounted on grommets in the airplane; it must be deeply bedded in foam packing for its immunity to the effects of vibration. The total assembly time for the receiver package and RF modules was about 8 hours spread over several days to avoid errors due to fatigue.

KIT SERVOS

The servo units were identical; the parts for one are shown in Fig. 8-9. The circuit parts for the servos were the most difficult to assemble because the decoder circuit board (Fig. 8-10) is so small, and the possibility of bridging conductive "islands" so great; here a magnifying glass was indispensable as a soldering aid. Frankly, I wouldn't blame you for copping out and buying assembled servos, the task is so tedious. (Larger servos are easier to build, however.)

One respondent to my survey said he potted (encapsulated) his servo decoder and receiver chassis in a silicon compound to prevent vibration problems; I didn't follow his lead, but it sounds like a worthwhile idea.

Following the completion of the electronics associated with the servos, dealing with the remainder of their innards,

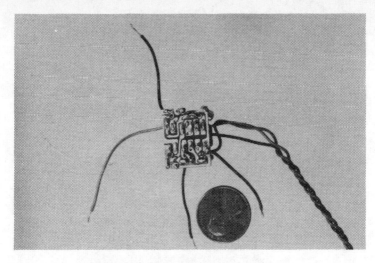

Fig. 8-10. Assembled servo decoder.

the motor and gears (Fig. 8-11), was quite straightforward. With the feedback potentiometer in place, its base centered so the wiper was positioned properly on the center of the resistive element, I installed the motor and soldered its leads. The unit as ready for packaging appears in Fig. 8-12. As you can see, taking the unit apart to clean or replace the potentiometer or motor would be quite simple; the gears are numbered, making assembly mistakes practically impossible.

Fig. 8-11. Locating the servo gears was relatively easy; they are identified by number.

Fig. 8-12. The completed servo assembly ready for encasement.

I had some trouble with the servo units. I must confess that after building two of the four needed, I became a little careless. The result was that the two remaining failed to work. I took my problem children to the nearby Heathkit repair center where I received every consideration and a solution to my troubles. Besides a motor wired backward (my fault), a

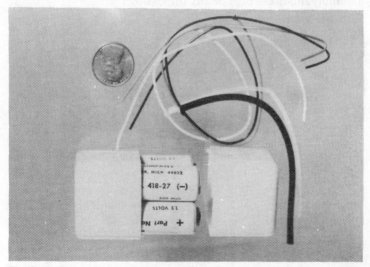

Fig. 8-13. Two of these battery packs are used in the transmitter; the case comes apart easily for cell replacement.

defective integrated circuit was discovered; it was quickly replaced without cost and connected for me in the unit so I could leave with an operating servo.

The testing and centering procedure for the servos essentially entails rotating the base of the feedback potentiometer until the servo arm is centered. A test circuit is included in this kit, which you build and connect between the receiver and servo with plugs and sockets; it produces a signal used to center the servo.

For the receiver, servo, and transmitter, three battery packs were furnished, one of which is shown in Fig. 8-13. The cells are soldered together in series to give 4.8 volts per pack; each cell's polarity is clearly marked. A separate charger with an isolation transformer is included in the kit for charging them. It also has to be assembled but goes together easily.

THE TRANSMITTER

Putting the transmitter parts (Fig. 8-14) together was the most time-consuming aspect of assembling the kit: 36 hours of accumulated time were spent on construction. Even though I took breaks often, and the construction details were clear enough, I often found myself believing I had read an instruction correctly, only to discover upon reading it again that I hadn't understood it the first time. So important is

Fig. 8-14. Transmitter and charger parts.

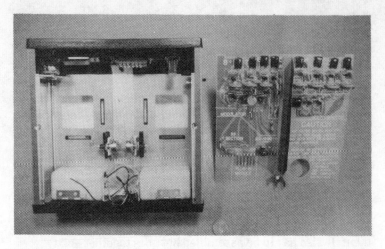

Fig. 8-15. Transmitter case with batteries installed (bottom) and completed circuit board.

understanding what you're reading when dealing with kit instructions, I suggest you rehearse what looks like a difficult or ambiguous step. It has also been my experience that people who get tired or anxious while building kits have a tendency to rely on drawings for instruction, or anticipate steps without reading about them. I'm sorry to say that I have to count myself among those people. Confronted with a task I thought to be a snap, and a nice line drawing to help me, I hurried and put a metal washer in the control-stick assembly where I should have used one made of Teflon; the error was discovered when I tried to make the parts fit. After reading the instructions

Fig. 8-16. Parts for one control-stick gimbal assembly.

130

again, following each word with the point of a pencil, and interrogating myself about what I had done, I found that the same haste that wasted some of my time also wasted the right part. I couldn't find a Teflon washer—not until a frantic search ended at a trash can where the right part lay concealed and alone in its plastic bag.

I again used my organizational procedure with the parts and verified the complement against the checklist provided. The construction was done in stages, the first being wiring the printed-circuit board (Fig. 8-15); a gutter dividing the circuit board houses the collapsed antenna.

Before I could install the transmitter chassis (PC board) in its case, I had to unite the parts for the control-stick gimbal assemblies (Fig. 8-16). The interconnecting cables, being precut and preassembled, were relatively easy to install; their placement in the case can be seen in Fig. 8-17.

After the cables were connected to the battery, switches, meter, control sticks, and the printed-circuit board, the case was closed; then it was on to the battery charger (shown in the upper right corner of Fig. 8-18, a photo of the completed RC system). No special equipment was needed to test the completed system. The transmitter meter, with the addition of

Fig. 8-17. Routing and connecting the transmitter cables was comparatively easy; all the wires are color-coded.

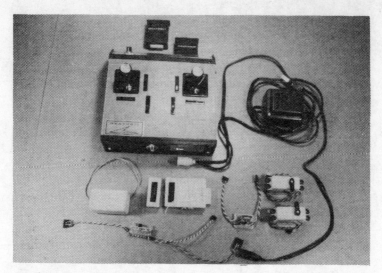

Fig. 8-18. The completed system performed admirably and gave an outstanding control range.

a resistor, was used to adjust both the transmitter and receiver.

I had a satisfactory RC system; all I needed was a model airplane to control: the topic of the chapter following.

9

Kit Models

The past decade has seen a vast improvement in RC models: in general they fly faster and their motors are more powerful; and there has been an improvement in the fuels they use. The approach to RC flying nowadays is more scientific and involves less guesswork on the part of the modeler. Although experimentation by the amateur aerodynamicist can contribute much to this field, the proliferation of excellent kits offered today makes it easy for the novice to realize his dreams of RC flight just hours after leaving a hobby shop. As was recommended for building an RC electronics system, I suggest a kit for your first plane.

KIT SELECTION

Modern model plane kits are available for various types of aircraft, each suited to the builder's individual taste and capabilities, whatever they may be. There are types for youngsters and novices, oldsters and veteran fliers. This hobby allows one to start from almost anywhere as far as the type of aircraft is concerned; advancement could lead to fast pylon racers, helicopters, and classic aircraft—but there's always a new challenge and excitement around the corner, no matter where you stand.

As a sample construction project, I chose a model that best fit the requirements for a beginner's first effort: one that

Fig. 9-1. Clear, detailed instructions are included with the kit for a Sig Kadet, a slow flying trainer.

would fly relatively slowly; one needing little power; one using simple, slab-sided construction; and one that comes with clear, detailed plans. The Sig Kadet, one of several planes having the desirable qualities outlined, was the one I picked. Figure 9-1 shows the kit before it is broken down into parts categories for the various construction steps.

Typical of a good kit, the Kadet comes with full-sized plans, an instruction booklet, all the necessary balsa parts stamped out of sheets, and hardware for the landing gear, moveable surfaces, and motor mounts. Not surprisingly, wheels, glue, dope, and covering materials were not included; these items, available at most hobby shops, are provided by the builder as a matter of course. The modeler must also obtain a small saw, sandpaper, and paints. A small vice is also helpful, as well as a few small-tipped screwdrivers, pliers, a drill, a right triangle to insure square sides and proper alignment, scissors, and a yardstick.

PREPARATIONS

Ideally, projects like this are undertaken in an unrestricted area, such as a vacant or nearly vacant garage equipped with a bench, cabinets, and a good assortment of tools. Better yet would be a separate workshop built of cement blocks; or one using a sturdy wood frame and siding, or a corrugated-steel hut with heating and air conditioning. But a room set aside for this kind of activity—say, in an attic or basement—and furnished with a fixed or fold-down bench would be more than adequate.

I considered building my kit in my office, alongside the typewriter, bookcases, file cabinets, and other space-consuming encumberances, including an antique brass bed; that bed became my workbench after I had covered it with a sheet of ¾-inch plywood. It worked out fine. If space is one of your problems, consider this approach. The main consideration in building a model is isolation, finding a place where parts in midassembly (especially those freshly glued) won't be disturbed; the space requirement is determined by the area of two wing halves, actually.

The work surface I used was good enough for laying out and tacking down wings, the first and most difficult procedure. Some modelers prefer cork board for this; special jigs for this aspect of plane construction can be obtained from a hobby shop.

GETTING STARTED

The wing ribs, stamped out of balsa sheeting, must be separated as shown in Fig. 9-2. They have to be trimmed to

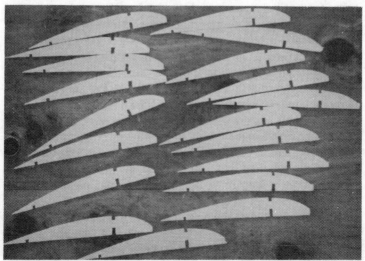

Fig. 9-2. Wing ribs after they have been pushed out of balsa sheet; next they must be trimmed.

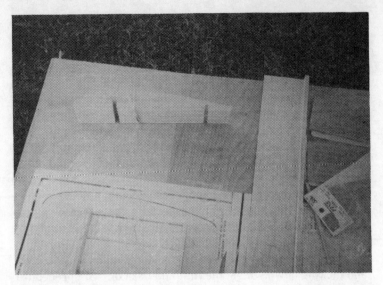

Fig. 9-3. Ribs ready to be glued in place; note how the slots in the bundled ribs align.

uniform length and smoothed; the slots that take the spars must align when the ribs are bundled. Care must be taken that the slots are not overwide; otherwise, spars might fit loosely. I try to cut the slots just a little under the width specified at first so they can be widened after a test for fit. When the ribs have been correctly cut and slightly sanded (Fig. 9-3), they are ready to be laid out on the main spar, which is pinned to the work surface directly over the plan. The use of plastic food wrap underneath is recommended to prevent glue from running down and joining the wing structure to the building plans; the wrap is laid over the plans and the spars and flat planking are put in place and pinned down securely.

If your kit has crooked spars (a company's quality-control department just can't catch every flaw) try steaming them and straightening them as they dry. If this doesn't work, you could make another trip to the hobby shop for new spars, but short of that, widen the rib slots so the spar can be slightly crooked without putting tension on the ribs. (Internal tension created at this stage can cause a wing to warp later, something that could take effort to straighten out.) If the ribs are too loose in places after the slots have been widened, glue a small piece of balsa sheet along the ribs to close the slots, but be careful of adding too much weight.

136

Figure 9-4 shows how the ribs of my D-sectioned (at the leading edge) wing halves are aligned before being glued. Joined, the halves comprise the wing depicted in Fig. 9-5.

When I first cut out the ribs, I made a template by tracing one, so I could make more in case a wing repair was necessary after flying the plane; it could also serve in building a new wing. I found that a thickness gauge was needed to measure unmarked pieces of balsa (the pieces marked were $1/32$, $1/16$, $1/8$, and $3/16$ -inch thick). I satisfied this need by getting some marked sample pieces of balsa from a hobby shop and using them for comparison.

Although the wing was ready for covering at this point, it was necessary to check it thoroughly for twists and to reglue the joints, each of which had to be checked for tightness of fit. I found it advantageous to go back over the glued joints and add extra glue to each; the added weight wasn't much, especially when compared to the advantage of being certain that the bond was strong.

The fuselage was relatively easy to build because it is slab-sided and is laid out right on the plans as was the wing. After the sides were cut (Fig. 9-6), I used a triangle to insure right angles as I assembled them at the cabin section. Then the tail was pulled together, held by rubber bands, and glued.

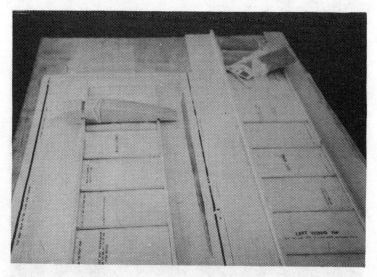

Fig. 9-4. The ribs are tested for fit along the spars before they are permanently installed.

Fig. 9-5. Joined; the combined wing sections are 58 inches long (the extra strip of wood in the photo is a yardstick).

Following this, the separators were put into place (Fig. 9-7) and glued.

Care must be taken to build on the plans for the right fuselage contour. Triangular gussets are installed against the

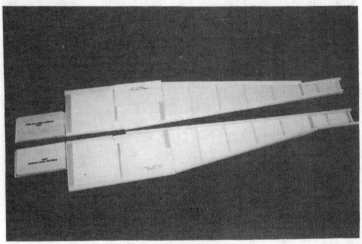

Fig. 9-6. Fuselage sides.

Fig. 9-7. Top view of fuselage showing triangular gussets (encircled).

upright at the rear of the cabin section (encircled in Fig. 9-7). This kind of bracing is useful in many places to insure strength; I added some to the nose section for that purpose.

The hardwood landing gear crossmember is placed across the open cabin bottom (Fig. 9-8); the small balsa stick in the photo is used to hold rubber bands in place.

The motor section has to be planned for fuel tank space. The tank (Fig. 9-9) consists of a plastic bottle and a plug with copper tubing inlets for air and fuel, and a flexible plastic tube weighted so it will remain immersed in fuel regardless of how gravity or centrifugal force might place it. Figure 9-10 shows the tank placed beside its compartment in the nose section; notice how the sides of the nose section have been

Fig. 9-8. Bottom view of fuselage following the addition of a hardwood landing gear strip (the one crossed by the small strip in the center of the photo).

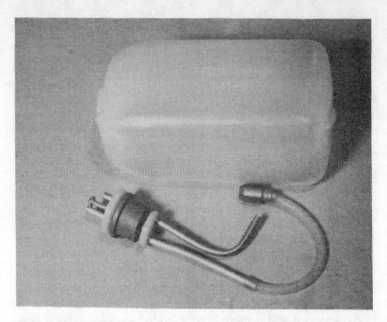

Fig. 9-9. Fuel tank assembly. The small fitting at one end of the plastic tubing stays submerged in fuel, regardless of its position in flight.

strengthened by the addition of quarter-inch balsa slabs. The next step is placing planks over the top *or* bottom of the fuselage (it must be left open on one side for the radio installation); I chose to leave the top open.

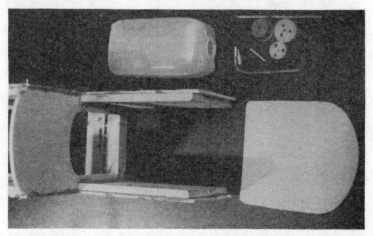

Fig. 9-10. The fuel tank next to its compartment in the nose section; batteries will go below it.

The landing gear is first fitted into holes drilled into each end of the hardwood landing gear block directly under the planking (Fig. 9-11). The landing gear halves were then wrapped with copper (bell) wire and soldered to form a sleeve, which was bolted to the hardwood block with small straps (furnished). The landing gear sections are supplied bent into the proper shape. After being fitted, the landing gear can be removed so its solid base can support the fuselage while further work is done on it.

At this point, my workbench/bed was fairly crowded with the subassemblies of a plane well on its way to completion (Fig. 9-12). During particularly lengthy breaks in the construction, I moved flammable compounds (such as dope) outside to their own special storage area for safety's sake. (If there are small children in your home, keep an eye on hazards like knives and razor blades.)

The motor mounts (aluminum) you see fastened to the firewall in Fig. 9-13 were included in the kit; two lines are drawn on the firewall: the vertical line represents the center of the fuselage; the horizontal one is an extension of the thrust line (both derived from the plans). These are necessary for correct engine alignment. The plane plans also recommended

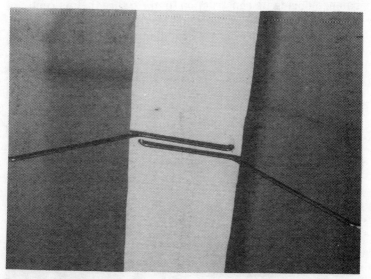

Fig. 9-11. Temporary installation of the landing gear on the bottom; the job is finished by wrapping the rods with wire; soldering them; then clamping the assembly in place.

Fig. 9-12. Work in progress on a bedroom workbench made by placing ¾-inch plywood over a bed.

drawing a line delineating the center of gravity and labeling it with an encircled X (Fig. 8-14). Space is left between the bulkhead and the engine so it can be adjusted to the correct angle of pitch.

It is important to keep a constant check on the plane's balance during its construction to make sure that its center of gravity doesn't get dislocated. You can move parts easily while testing the balance by holding the fuselage with your

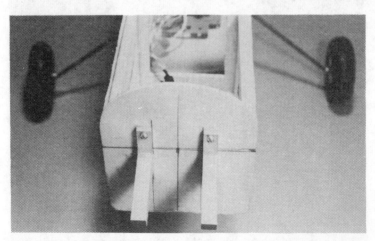

Fig. 9-13. Motor mounts in place. The vertical line is the fuselage's center; it is crossed by the thrust line.

Fig. 9-14. The engine is mounted slightly away from the bulkhead so it can be adjusted for the proper pitch (angled, if need be); the encircled X on the fuselage is the center of gravity as given by the plans.

thumb and middle finger on the center of gravity marks (one on each side). Weight can be added to achieve the desired balance, but this must be forestalled until the plane is finally covered and doped. Making a trial assembly (Fig. 9-15) can give you the feeling that you are really making some headway with the project.

This is a time to concentrate on not being overanxious. The RC installation, the covering procedure, removing warps from

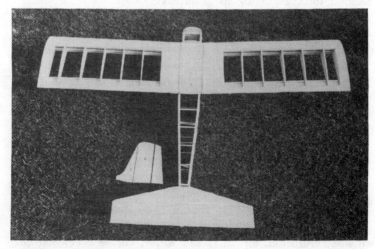

Fig. 9-15. A trial assembly before the hardware is included gives a good idea of what the finished plane will look like.

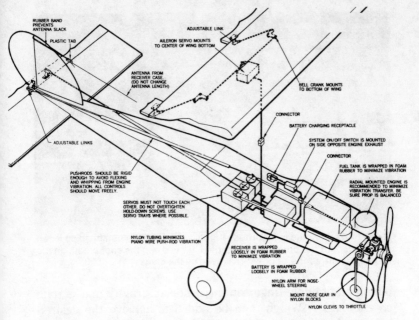

Fig. 9-16. Typical airborne RC installation. (Courtesy Kraft Systems, Inc.)

the wing—all these steps are yet to come. Then, too, it may be necessary to sand and fill rough spots for best airflow around the plane. The same company that produces my kit also makes a putty (epoxy) for this; it hardens to a surface that can be sanded, thus disguising any amateurish work.

INSTALLING THE RC PAYLOAD

My airplane does not have ailerons; the controls are limited to rudder, elevator, and motor. Many believe that one might as well have ailerons to begin with. If this is what you want, then a kit like the Sig Kommander, a *trainer* that can accommodate four control channels, would be a good first choice. I opted for a less complicated model to get a feel for flying again before going into something that might be tricky to control. (I also see it as a hand-me-down—barring its wreckage— for my grandsons, who will want to try their hand at flying soon, I'm sure.)

For a radio-control installation to be acceptable, it must be properly balanced, have sturdy mountings, and be protected against vibration, oil, dirt, and water, yet be accessible for servicing or removal; the associated pushrods must be unrestricted in their movement. Figure 9-16 shows a typical four-channel RC installation. Notice that the servo controlling the rudder (one of three placed inline across the fuselage) also moves the nose wheel. The fourth servo, located in the center of the wing, activates the aileron through bell cranks, but the connections between pushrods and ailerons can also be made directly, as shown in Fig. 9-17. (Notice how this arrangement makes one aileron deflect downward while the other goes up.)

Because the receiver I had built was not compatible with the limited controls my first plane was to have (it was an eight-channel rig, remember), I chose a receiver/servo package: some of those so-called little red bricks (referring to squarish, modular design) made by EK Logictrol (Fig. 9-18). The elevator and rudder servos are encased together, while the motor-control unit is outboard. As was expected, this arrangement made the installation a relative snap. The double-duty unit is shown on a $\frac{1}{16}$-inch mounting board, which was cut using measurements taken of the plane's cabin area per instructions given in the plan. Of course, the

Fig. 9-17. The control arm of the wing-mounted servo moves the ailerons in complementary directions for turns in flight.

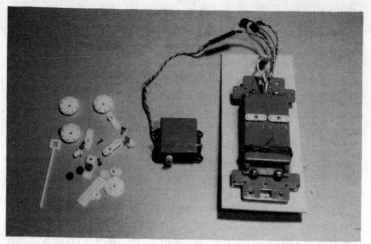

Fig. 9-18. The mounting board (right) holds the receiver and serves for elevator and rudder control; the outboard unit is the motor-control servo.

recommendation given by the plane manufacturer as to the location of the radio-control equipment was only general in nature; the plane maker has no way of knowing what electronic gear will be used with its product. The wire wrapped around the receiver, its antenna, will be stretched back to the vertical stabilizer. Rubber grommets and plastic fittings are supplied to reduce vibration to an acceptable level. The various cams, wheels, grommets, and other hardware supplied are for mounting the units, and for directing the motion of the servos' outputs; you can use a wheel output that will give connection points 45° apart around its circumference.

I added the motor mounts, motor, and propeller next and found that the plane was balanced as it should have been. The fuel tank with its stopper in place fit nicely, its centerline aligned with the throttle pushrod; assembly and installation work was going very smoothly.

Although it wasn't included at this point, I planned to have quick access to the battery pack, for its removal, by using a small door in the underside of the fuselage near the front cabin bulkhead.

The receiver package support board was placed on its crossmembers and temporarily held in place with pins so I could adjust its height; it has to be below the thrust line on the fuselage.

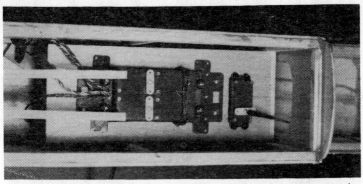

Fig. 9-19. Two balsa pushrods (left) will be connected to servo arms by means of threaded wire fittings; even without the fuel tank, the plane can be balanced at this stage.

PUSHROD HOOKUP

The balsa pushrods shown running to the back of the fuselage (left) in Fig. 9-19 receive wire tips that are threaded so small adjustments of the control surfaces can be made following a test flight. Other planes use flexible cables sheathed in plastic tubing; their ends are soldered to fittings (and a few inches behind the fittings to keep the cable from unravelling), which connect to servo arms and attachment points on the control surfaces. When using an angular device that changes the direction of a servo arm's motion, as for ailerons, be sure that its bearing is long enough and solid enough so the linkage element won't turn slightly, bend and, therefore, bind. Figure 9-20 shows the wire extensions of

Fig. 9-20. Pushrod connections to control surfaces.

Fig. 9-21. My completed Kadet kit, ready to fly.

pushrods fitted with clevises, which are attached to fittings on the control surfaces called *horns*.

FINAL TOUCHES

The plane was ready for covering. This was done by sanding the surfaces as smooth as possible, followed by two coats of clear dope (an adhesive). After the dope had dried, it was sanded lightly with very fine sandpaper to facilitate covering the plane with silk. The silk had to be cut into pieces (four for the wing, five for the fuselage, two for the rudder, and two for the stabilizer) that were oversize by an inch. Each piece, in turn wetted and laid in place, was pulled taut (but gently) to take out wrinkles, while the edges were tacked down with dope. Then more dope was applied, using my fingers and excess silk was trimmed. Ideally, silk should be applied as squarely as possible, that is, with the fabric threads running parallel with the major axes of the part being covered, then worked smooth. As the silk dries, it shrinks, drawing itself tightly against the framework. During the doping process, wing warps are removed by twisting the wing in the direction opposite of the warp as the dope dries; this is another area in which assistance may be needed.

The end result of the project, painted and ready to fly, is shown in Fig. 9-21.

I found aliphatic-resin glues quite amenable to work with in that they are comparatively odorless, they dry reasonably fast, and they bond tightly. The particular glue I used, Sig

148

Bond, is dopeproof, fuelproof, and can be sanded very smooth. Any comparable glue will do just as well, as long as the model is constructed to last a long time.

Too many modelers, when starting with their first kit, treat it as something expendable; they just throw it together for the experience, expecting to lose it with the rationale that they will do better with the next one. This can establish a pattern of shoddy construction habits. I hope you'll build your first plane as though it were to be your last and only one; besides the pride of workmanship it will give you, this approach will save you the expense of aircraft damage.

ALTERNATE KITS

If you're so anxious to get something into the air that you don't want to devote the construction time necessary for the

Fig. 9-22. This pilot (E. L. Safford, IV) is learning the fundamentals of aerodynamics with a rubber-band powered model.

Fig. 9-23. The light, protruding member in the wing section (center) is an open glider spoiler.

kind of kit described, consider a ready-to-fly kit. All you have to do is put on the control surfaces, install the RC system, break in the motor—and you're ready to fly. Some models even come with the necessary radio gear. If you consider your son or daughter to young to be trusted with gasoline engines, starting equipment, and radio-transmission gear, a rubber-band powered model might be the way to go; they use essentially the same type of construction as the larger models (Fig. 9-22) but are so cheap as to be considered expendable.

Many have found that flying RC gliders is an excellent way to have fun in this hobby while reducing the chances of bad crack-ups. However, because their wings are usually much longer and lighter than those used for powered craft, they are more difficult to build without warps (unless you are extremely careful). Launching a glider requires a winch, tow car, or other device to get it into the air; and once it's up, its performance will depend on you finding thermals for a reasonable flight duration.

Controls for gliders are about the same as for airplanes. Because gliders fly slower, spoilers are often used in the wing and tail to give the same control effects that ailerons and elevators produce in powered planes. Figure 9-23 shows a glider wing with an open spoiler.

PROGRESSIVE KITS

I was curious about the other various models produced by the company that made the one under discussion so far, specifically, how they differed in the demands they make on a modeler's skill as a builder and flyer. The best source for this information, of course, is the planes' designer, so I queried Sig's Claude McCullough. He said the Kadet is good for a beginner because of its inherent stability; it will practically fly itself. If you stop giving radio commands, it will fly on undistrubed. The low, nearly symmetrical wind seen on shunt or pylon-racing planes has virtually no interent stability; continual pilot guidance is necessary to keep it straight and level in flight. If radio contact is broken or delayed, it is only a matter of seconds before these models will dip their wing or nose. The jump from the Kadet to something more advanced is a big one. Any delay in control at the wrong moment can wreck a low-winged airplane because the flier will have a difficult time trying to regain control.

In response to an additional question about the Kadet's lack of ailerons, Claude commented that they would be of little assistance because the plane's inherent stability makes it slow to react; furthermore, it wouldn't provide the necessary increase in the training pace. Rather than thinking in terms of modifying the Kadet, McCullough suggests a Kommander, an intermediate design. It flies much faster than the Kadet, but not as fast as an advanced, stunt design. It has more inherent stability than a low-winged "stunter," but not so much that it hampers maneuverability; yet it gives the novice a little time to think and allows some reaction-time lag. The wing section is semisymmetrical: halfway between the high-lift and slow, stable airfoil on the Kadet, and the fully symmetrical wing of the Komet, the next step up.

Claude also added that when you fly something like the Kadet (sans ailerons), it is important to use the stick configuration the same way you would with an aileron equipped plane. In other words, the rudder servo stick in a four-channel outfit is not the one to use for the rudder in a three-channel airplane. This means that you have to plug the rudder servo of the Kadet into the aileron channel of the (four-channel) receiver, so when you make the transition to the Kommander or Komet (or their equivalents), the stick movement you have become used to for flying left and right will be the same on the transmitter; but in the airplane, it will operate the ailerons. (Rudder is used little in turning an aileron equipped airplane. It is mainly used during takeoffs and for special maneuvers requiring rudder action, such as spins, wingovers, and corrections added during point rolls.)

CONSTRUCTION TIPS

There are several measures you can take toward acheiving success in building your first model plane, whether it is a trainer or an intermediate design. Some, like those that apply to assembling the electronics for radio control, might seem so simplistic and obvious as to go without mention. But you'd be surprised how many, in their (understandable) haste, toss common sense aside and disregard even the most matter-of-fact precautions. Distilled from my experience and that of others, the tips that follow should see you through your first RC model project to a rewarding conclusion:

- Study the plans and parts before you begin; try to get an idea of how to pace your work.
- Get everything you're going to need ahead of time (frantic drives to the hobby shop not only waste valuable construction time, they can be dangerous).
- Follow instructions; don't rely on the drawings for the procedure.
- Take your time and keep your work area clear of tools and materials you won't be using.
- Check and double-check ongoing construction against the plans.
- Keep the plane as light as possible; if you think certain areas need reinforcement, check the feasibility of adding the extra weight with someone who has had experience with your particular model.
- Preglue all joints and make sure parts fit properly before gluing them.

10

Flight-Field-Fliers

Now comes the proof of the pudding: Will your plane fly? If you're new to the sport, you may also wonder how to get it into the air, and what to do with it once it's up. More important than these considerations is the question of *where* you're going to fly it.

If your neighborhood isn't so populated with RC enthusiasts that you can locate a flying field by turning your ear toward the sound of droning minimotors, try to find a suitable site through your hobby dealer; the Academy of Model Aeronautics might also be able to help through their directory of clubs. However you find the nearest field, when you get there you will find some of the nicest, friendliest, and most capable hobbyists you'll ever want to meet.

YOUR FLYING FIELD COMPANIONS

Who are they, those people in vacation clothes, wearing funny hats and colorful shirts, who are strolling about the field or standing over their models? This information is also included among the results of my survey. You will no doubt note that in the list of occupations that follows, a great many professions are given; perhaps this fact says more about RC hobbyists than any other. The occupations submitted by my respondents are: chiropractor, sales manager, land developer, research technician, research biochemist, retired army officer, chemistry professor, chemical engineer, computer installation planner, perodonist, auto truck painter, mechanical engineer, automotive engineer, art professor, ship builder, aeronautical engineer, airline pilot, quality-control technician, police officer, machinist, automotive job setter, senior engineer draftsman, environmental scientist, hair stylist, USAF pilot, office manager, avionics technician, purchasing supervisor, welder, tool and die maker, business machines field engineer, telephone repairman, high school teacher, credit bureau manager, railroad employee, civil service instructor, director of college drafting department, apparel store president, electronics field engineer, electrical engineer, electrical contractor, auto parts manager, electrical engineering superviser, operations research analyist, postal supervisor, junior high school teacher, casuality insurance agent, typewriter repairman, military officer, enlisted military man, minister, apartment maintenance man, architect, bank assistant vice-president, engraver, aircraft mechanic, gas utility manager, nuclear physicist, control systems engineer, construction engineer, war veteran, air conditioning contractor, pharmacist, attorney, hobby shop manager, appliance repair technician, microelectronics researcher, oil company operations supervisor, elementary school teacher, real estate broker, sheetmetal worker, banker, farmer, crane operator, farm equipment production coordinator, advertising executive, air traffic controller, petroleum engineer, government nuclear specialist, fireman, plant manager, mechanic, physician, truck driver, engineering model maker, accountant, cabinetmaker, senior structures engineer, construction worker, car dealer, author, photographer, and several students in high school and college.

The people represented by this list have found a common interest in radio-controlled model airplanes. One of them related his entry into the hobby: "I found myself going home from the office night after night, watching television, and going to bed, a routine. Eventually I said 'to heck with this; it makes a man old fast.' So I began building RC model airplanes. I now have a wonderful time building scale models—I love it. My children enjoy it also."

So these are the RC flyers, people who beat the doldrums of modern living, the ones you see at flying fields on Sunday afternoons for fly-ins, or during the evening at sport-flying events; get to know them.

The range of occupations given comes with a range of incomes, naturally—but they also denote the investment range in RC equipment.

FLYING COSTS

I never said the hobby was cheap. You may have to start gradually at first, especially if you are feeling a financial crunch; this might hit home if you are a student. If this is the case, think about building a full complement of RC gear sequentially: an airplane, a motor, then a control system. Clubs can help make easing into the hobby as painless as possible; and they can be an outlet for good used equipment, equipment in good working order that is being abandoned in favor of the latest models.

"But how much is it going to cost in the long run?" you might ask. Read what a respondent in Maine had to say: "As of January 6, 1975, I have made 460 flights with 15 airplanes. I still have 4 of the 15; I retired two and lost several due to radio problems. My total flight time is 44 hours 35 minutes; I made 459 landings. My total equipment cost is $2,905.97. Thus the cost per flight was $6.32. I have 2 transmitters, 3 receivers, 16 servos, 4 working planes, 4 partially built planes, and 10 engines: a 0.4, a 0.46, a 0.49, and 70.6s." (The specifications refer to CID.)

Now before you decide to chuck it, let me say that some respondents have less than $500 invested in their hobby—and have flown for years (flying one airplane and using one control system they were very careful with). The average investment, however, is a little over $2000; the largest figure is $10,000; and the least spent, $350. (The largest figure includes the cost of tools and other attendent equipment.)

To round out this picture of the RC modeler, I include his age: the oldest is 64; the youngest, 15; the average, 40 plus.

YOUR PLANE'S DEBUT

Once you've found a flying field, even if it is a converted cow pasture like the one shown in Fig. 10-1, wait for a relatively calm day for your try at flight. This doesn't mean there should be no wind; the wind just shouldn't be gusty. (A steady, gentle wind is ideal.) Initial trim is accomplished by

Fig. 10-1. Coming in for a landing on a converted cow pasture. It took some effort on the part of all concerned to surface this runway.

performing a glide test first; this will also give an idea of what the plane's flight characteristics are.

With the radio equipment off, the control surfaces in their neutral positions, the propeller removed, and the motor wrapped in cloth to keep dirt out, hold the plane from below, at or a little behind the balance point. Run into the wind and push the plane forward and down slightly the moment you feel it start to lift from your hand. Watch what happens and compare the action to the glide test results analysis given in Fig. 10-2.

When you have adjusted the airplane so it glides straight, slightly downward, and relatively fast, and comes down on its wheels in an acceptable landing, you are ready for a powered flight attempt—well, almost.

Before making the attempt, you'll have to make a radio range check. Have someone operate your transmitter in response to you giving hand signals for left and right rudder, up and down elevator, and fast and slow throttle as you walk away, carrying the airplane with its motor running. You should be able to walk 100 yards or further from the transmitter and have the plane respond to all your control signals. Should the plane fail to respond before you reach the 100-yard mark, some adjustments to the RC equipment will have to be made; this may be as simple as correcting your

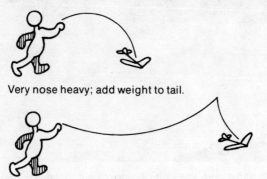

Very nose heavy; add weight to tail.

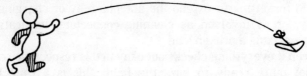

Tail heavy or thrown too hard into wind, a plane will stall.

Slightly nose heavy, try adding shim to elevator panel—generally do not look for a float-glide.

Good: straight, fast glide (do all testing with neutral rudder).

Fast but tricky may indicate wing warp.

Some degree of turn with neutral rudder: elevation not positioned correctly, wing warp, or vertical fin not centered on fuselage.

Fig. 10-2. Test-glide analysis.

Fig. 10-3. With enough power, this plane (taking off) will continue to climb, then level off.

error in forgetting to extend the antenna fully or charging a battery, or as involved as cleaning connectors, lubricating servos, or fixing a broken lead.

Even if everything checks out okay in this respect, you are still not quite ready to buzz the field; this is a time for reflection.

You should always have a plan of what you are going to try to do once getting your model airborne is imminent, no matter what kind of craft it is. Some flyers say the best way to start is to rev the motor slightly and taxi the plane around the flying field while you steer it and adjust the motor control until you get a feel for the radio system. The only argument against this approach is that control of a steerable nose operating in conjunction with a rudder is apt to be slower than when the airplane is airborne. Taxiing, however, will give you a feel for controlling your airplane. When you can taxi straight at a reasonable speed, you are ready to try a takeoff and flight (assuming you have trimmed the model according to glide-test results).

If you're ready, send the airplane smoothly down the runway, straight into the wind, and advance the throttle rather quickly, so the model lifts off and begins a slow climb. If the model goes fast down the runway but doesn't look as though it will leave the ground, a little up elevator may be required. Don't try to get the plane into the air as fast as you might see other, more proficient pilots doing. This takes skill, judgment born of experience, and a good knowledge of the airplane and its motor. The veteran flier knows by instinct exactly when to level off by commanding down elevator at the right time to gain flying speed comfortably. You don't have time to stop and think during this kind of maneuver. A delay can mean a crash. Once you know your airplane and know how it reacts to commands, you will be able to accomplish this maneuver. There are reasons for using it: to get the airplane into the air quickly to minimize the effects of wind gusts, and to avoid rough spots on the runway that might cause the model to turn unexpectedly or bounce. Full throttle and up elevator the moment the plane gains flying speed, followed by a little down elevator to prevent a stall, then up elevator again to get to flying altitude while keeping the model straight, using the rudder or aileron control as necessary for a smooth takeoff culminating in satisfactory flight. Figure 10-3 shows the kind of takeoff to expect from a properly trimmed plane.

If your plane isn't too heavy, you can hand launch it. This is done in the same manner as a glide test: launch it by pushing it forward or slightly downward; it will fly and begin to climb by itself—if it is properly trimmed. (Don't throw the plane upward; it could flip over and crash behind you.) If it moves straight away from you in level flight, command a little up elevator to make it climb slowly; Fig. 10-4 describes hand-launch effects and how to correct adverse ones. Another variation on taking off entails attaching a string to the plane's tail wheel. Stand on the string and rev the motor to full speed. When you're sure the motor will run without faltering, position your hands on the transmitter controls and lift your foot; the airplane will shoot down the runway and into the air. This method allows you to keep both hands on the controls during takeoff.

Once the model is high enough, you can begin controlling it fully, but do not change the motor speed (the throttle should be wide open).

MANEUVERS

Plane maneuvers involving left or right turns only correspond to control stick movements when the plane is going away from you. To avoid having to think backward, so to speak, as your plane approaches, turn your back to it so the plane's left will be your left and your right, its right. Although you will have to crane your neck while doing this, it will make steering easy and help you to avoid mistakes, especially

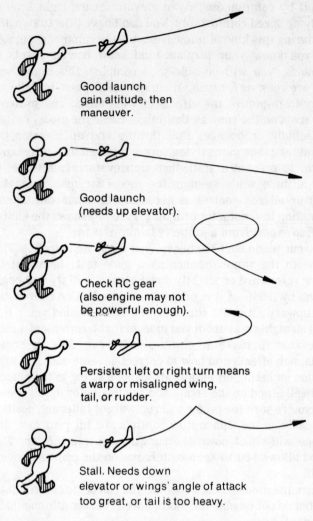

Good launch
gain altitude, then
maneuver.

Good launch
(needs up elevator).

Check RC gear
(also engine may not
be powerful enough).

Persistent left or right turn means
a warp or misaligned wing,
tail, or rudder.

Stall. Needs down
elevator or wings' angle of attack
too great, or tail is too heavy.

Fig. 10-4. Hand-launch effects.

during landings. Once you gain experience, you may be able to abandon this procedure.

Never give a full control signal unless you are certain the situation demands it. Send signals for gentle turns, for slow climbs and gradual loss of altitude. It might be helpful to practice imaginary landings in the sky by making the plane "touch down" on the horizon so you can acquire the judgment needed for the real thing. The more you fly, the more you'll learn about your airplane and its personality, its attributes and peculiarities. The fact that each airplane is different is one reason they are so much fun, and why modelers have so many kinds of planes (or so many models of the same airplane).

LANDING

Landings should be made into the wind. Make your plane circle overhead but slightly downwind of you, then bring it in while watching how fast it loses altitude. To make the plane drop faster or glide further, use the elevator control—but very carefully by adjusting it in small increments; this is especially important to avoid a stall when the motor has run out of fuel. Often, just before touching down, a plane will experience a little additional lift because of the *ground effect*: an interaction between the wing's downwash and the ground; this can cause your plane to glide further than you expect it to. Some fliers suggest making initial landings in tall grass (Fig. 10-5) as a precaution against possible damage.

Some say that when you are landing slowly, you can rev the engine and try again, if the first approach looks questionable. But this touch-and-go landing method is difficult even for seasoned RC pilots and shouldn't be counted on for

Fig. 10-5. Landing in grass can greatly reduce the risk of plane damage.

Fig. 10-6. The scene at a Sunday fly-in.

success by the novice. It's better to let the plane land—just get it down safely—even if it's a long way from your target spot on the field.

One of my respondents suggested painting the fuselage black and the wing yellow, so the plane's turns can be seen from a distance. (This is particularly useful if you're nearsighted; besides, special colors and designs can help you pick out your plane among others.)

CONTESTS

Once you've mastered the basic flying techniques, you could be ready for a Sunday fly-in contest. The range of difficulty involved can be quite broad.

I toured a flying field recently (it was a Sunday) so I could report on the scene you might see on your first visit and was immediately impressed by how little noise could be heard, even when two models were in the air at the same time. It seems that most modelers nowadays equip their planes with mufflers; the days of screaming minimotors seem to have passed. Some of the spectators had portable, briquette hot dog cookers, and drinks were available to all from a cooler. People lounged on folding chairs in the shade of brightly colored canopies (Fig. 10-6) watching the fun of a contest underway.

Each contestant took three turns at picking a card from a series of cards in a box. The face of each card described a flight maneuver the entrant had to perform. For example, one contestant's card directed him to start his engine, take off, circle the field, do a slow roll during the straight portion of the flight, and come in for a landing within a small circle painted

162

on the field—all within 3 minutes as verified by an official timer (Fig. 10-7).

Points were awarded for each stage of the flight. Then the contestant left the runway to wait for his turn at the next maneuver described on another card. When each competitor had completed three such events—never knowing what maneuvers he might be required to perform—his score was averaged and compared to that of others. This is one type of Sunday fly-in contest, friendly competition in which everyone has fun and gets to fly. Pylon racing is usually a club activity. In this event, small sleek aircraft, glossy and carefully constructed, attain speeds between 150 and 180 mph as they race from one end of a field to the other, some minus their mufflers for greatest speed. The airplanes used for this competition (Fig. 10-8) have to be nearly perfect, that is, without blemishes, scars, or loose joints; and the equipment inside must be cushioned to withstand forces of up to 30Gx. The strain on mounting brackets, screws, bolts, and grommets—each part of the whole structure—is almost unbelievable. Wings, being particularly susceptible to this kind of punishment, are often lost immediately.

Pylon racing is considered the ultimate test of a pilot's expertise and of his plane's airworthiness. If the pilot experiences just one moment of hesitation or indecision, his plane can dive and crash in the blink of an eye—at the speeds

Fig. 10-7. The official timer for contests logs in entrants' names and gives them a starting time.

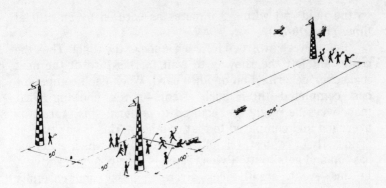

Fig. 10-8. Ten laps are made in a pylon race for a total distance of 2½ miles; flagmen at the single (scatter) pylon signals turns; turning short of it adds a lap to the offending pilot's course, and two such violations mean disqualification. (Courtesy National Miniature Pylon Racing Association.)

attained during this event, planes can be rendered unsalvageable.

Although my research discloses that many adults over 50 are engaged in the hobby, it seems (according to the statistics) that it is the younger pilots who excel at controlling the lightning fast airplanes seen at pylon-racing events. However, they rely on their *callers*, usually older persons, telling them when to turn and when there is another plane nearby. The flier must have nerves of steel, the eyes of an eagle, and all those other metaphoric attributes bestowed on pilots of full-sized planes; in other words, he's a pro. As if the tremendous speeds weren't enough to deal with—you can imagine what they would be, brought up to full scale—the pilots also have to contend with not just another rival in the air but many. In a less hectic vein, there are free-flight contests in which planes with very small (easily depleted) fuel tanks are made to take off nearly vertically to gain altitude fast; a minute or two later, the engine is starved (or a timing device spoils the plane's lift) and the plane glides—without control—for as long as possible. The fliers who specialize in this activity represent 7.23% of those who responded to my survey. Many of them are youngsters or newcomers to the field who are using this event in their study of the rudiments of aerodynamics.

If you're a competitive person, I suggest you become a member of the Academy of Model Aeronautics (806 15th St. NW., Washington D.C. 20005). The advantage? You will receive a copy of the official model aircraft regulations, which include descriptions of all recognized contest maneuvers (Fig. 10-9) and how they are judged in competition. Even if you aren't a member, you can obtain a copy of the booklet for a small charge. It will give all the flight information you'll need to get started, and enough to prepare you for contests.

FLYING INDOORS

For indoor types, there's indoor flying, an aspect of the sport showing a rather poor representation in my survey but one that is gaining in popularity. Flying indoors requires a tiny airplane that uses a carbon dioxide or electric motor for power. Because lift is hard to come by (there is no wind), special electronic subminiaturization techniques must be employed in making the attendant radio gear to make the payload as little as possible. This is one area in which hobbyists are hard at work supplementing the research being done by RC manufacturers. Exemplary of that ilk is Joe Clements, perhaps one of the foremost experimenters in indoor RC flight.

I discussed his airplanes with him. His first indoor model, built in 1972, was a 23-inch (wingspan) cabin model weighing only 2.65 ounces (complete). Powered by a CO_2 (carbon dioxide) engine, it flew both indoors and outdoors. His second model had a wingspan of 29 inches, yet its weight was reduced to only 2 ounces; it could not be used outdoors because its weight made it too sensitive to even the slightest wind (it flew fine indoors).

For his third attempt in this field, Clements designed a model with a 16-inch wingspan—and it weighed a mere 1.6 ounces. The CO_2 engine, a Brown 0.005, was the same size he used previously. His radio-control receiver, a stock Alben, controlled a smaller than normal-sized Benert actuator for rudder movement. (The actuator is a unit that is pulsed to cause the rudder to flop back and forth; if it is made to stay longer in one position than the other, the model turns in that direction.)

Joe indicated that he sees a bright future for this kind of airplane. He envisions a "chip" receiver using a 3-volt supply, and an actuator so small, it can be integral with the rudder; an airplane so equipped could weigh no more than an ounce. Demand, as always, will result in commercial products for indoor RC flight, but for the time being, it's every man for himself and every experimenter on his own.

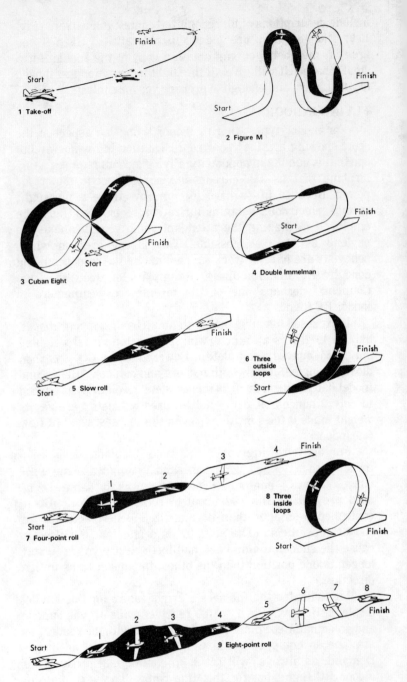

1 Take-off

2 Figure M

3 Cuban Eight

4 Double Immelman

5 Slow roll

6 Three outside loops

7 Four-point roll

8 Three inside loops

9 Eight-point roll

Fig. 10-9A. Basic radio-controlled flight maneuvers.

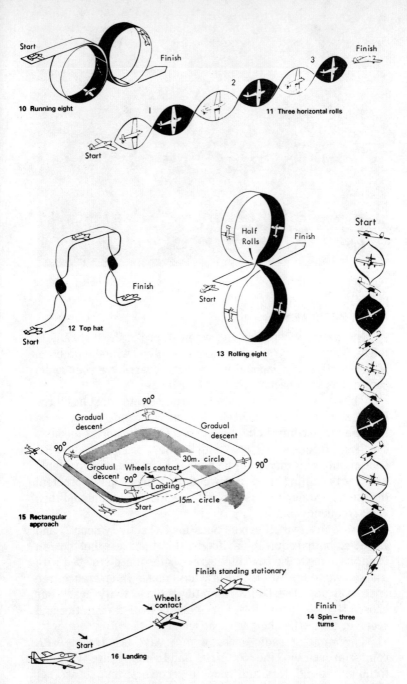

Fig. 10-9B. Advanced radio-controlled flight maneuvers. (Courtesy AMA.)

167

Fig. 10-10. Transmitters in an impound area while their owners await a clear channel.

COINTERFERENCE

No matter where you fly, when you're in the company of fellow fliers, you're going to have to contend with the problem of *cointerference*: basically, someone overriding your radio commands because he's on your frequency.

The contemporary RC model airplane enthusiast has three frequency bands and a heck of a lot of channels (not to be confused with control channel, *channel* in this context means a specific frequency) on which he can operate RC equipment—and more will be needed soon, the ones available now are becoming so overcrowded. It is sometimes a problem for the newcomer to this hobby to decide what band and then what frequency to use.

There are two citizen's bands for RC activity near 27 and 72 MHz, both requiring a license for their use but not an examination. Of the two, the former is the more crowded with users' communications. For the most interference-free operation on these bands, monitor radio activity near your chosen flying site and select crystals for your transmitter and receiver for the frequencies used least.

The amateur radio operator may have less trouble with cointerference on the 53 MHz band; many use variable frequency oscillators and tunable receivers, and so are not relegated to a crystal-controlled frequency.

168

FREQUENCY CONTROL

Most RC clubs use the 72 MHz band and have a frequency controller, someone assigned or elected to see that modelers on the same frequency don't interfere with each other. This is accomplished by using a frequency color code: each modeler is given a colored flag or streamer for his transmitter antenna that represents a specific frequency as determined by the AMA. Most flying fields have an area in which all transmitters are impounded (Fig. 10-10) before clearance is given for their use. This is understandable, especially when you consider that the most innocent of equipment checks made by one modeler can cause another's plane to crash. However, during informal meets, such as a Sunday fly-in, only colored flags may be impounded. Often, rather than flags, painted closthespins are used (Fig. 10-11).

However this system is implemented, each modeler must go to the impound area for the marker corresponding to the frequency he is using before he can fly; if the marker is

Fig. 10-11. Besides colored flags and streamers, clothespins (one is attached to the base of the antenna in this picture) are used to denote the frequency being used.

Fig. 10-12. The plane in the foreground of this picture (marked U.S. AIR FORCE) became the subject of a photo session involving prearranged maneuvers.

unavailable, it means the represented frequency is being used. The colors for the various bands and frequencies for RC use appear in Appendix C. Of course, when only a few go out to a field for an evening event of just a few flights, circumstances under which no officials are present, you can find out from everyone else what frequencies they are using to protect them and yourself.

PREFLIGHT INSPECTIONS

The wait for your turn to fly, rather than being irksome, gives you an opportunity to meet others and examine their models. It's also a good time to note the flying techniques used by your fellow fliers. And while you're waiting, check your plane and RC gear; this is the most you can do to insure success when your turn comes.

Having a plane that has worked consistently well for you time after time, doesn't mean it will give unerringly good performance without you giving attention to its condition. Although I am not one to capitalize on the misfortunes of others, I witnessed the sort of accident that can result from a flier's inattentiveness, one that I was able to document photographically. The model in question is the one shown nearest the camera, on the flight line in Fig. 10-12. I asked its

Fig. 10-13. A perfect takeoff; straight down the runway—the result of perfect trim and excellent pilot control.

owner, for the purpose of illustration, if he would control it for various maneuvers while I photographed it. He was agreeable, and shortly after it took off (Fig. 10-13), it came by for a low pass as I stood ready on the runway (Fig. 10-14). The dummy head in the cockpit took on human dimensions, the plane seemed so real. Manipulating his transmitter controls deftly, my confederate took his plane sky high in a nearly vertical climb, made it loop, and brought it back overhead (Fig. 10-15). As the plane circled the field for an approach to a very fast low-altitude pass, it failed to respond to its owner's command of up elevator and rammed into a fence; Fig. 10-16 shows the accident scene seconds after my arrival.

Fig. 10-14. During a low pass, this plane is so realistic one can almost imagine the (dummy) pilot's head moving.

Fig. 10-15. In a photo like this one; it is impossible to tell whether the plane is real or not, or how high it is.

I concurred with the pilot that the most obvious clue to the cause of the mishap was a broken elevator servo arm (encircled in Fig. 10-17). To both of us it seemed likely that the associated pushrod was binding in its plastic sleeve and

Fig. 10-16. The photo session that began with this plane's perfect takeoff couldn't, unfortunately, be concluded with a picture-perfect landing.

eventually froze; it was one of those cases of an irresistible force trying to overcome an immovable object: the torquey little servo just keep pulling until its arm broke.

Whenever you have a free moment to do so, make sure your linkages are free, installed so that constant flying will not cause the rubbing away of supports that can lead to binding. Straight pushrod runs, where possible, are best. I prefer that rigid rods move control surfaces; of course, in some cases, this arrangement just isn't possible. For a nose wheel or throttle, you may have to use tubing and flexible cable to get around fuel tanks, batteries, and other obstacles. But constant inspection of pushrods will pay dividends in trouble free flying. (The only thing I can offer in the way of a happy ending to the accident related is that the motor and receiver were unharmed.)

FIELD SAFETY

Not unlike many such organizations, the DCRC club has suggested safety rules regarding flying-field activity; the following has been gleaned from one of its newsletters:

- Use a starter if you have one; but never make connections to the glow plug until you have "flip-chocked" the engine.

Fig. 10-17. The loss of control that led to this scene is obviously the cause of a broken servo arm (encircled); how it broke is a matter of safe conjecture: a binding pushrod.

173

- Lacking a starter, use a "chicken stick" or other finger guard; in lieu of this, use a 2-inch length of ⅝- or ¾-inch (inside diameter) garden hose slit lengthwise to fit over your finger.

- Keep your head away from the (spinning) propeller while you adjust the carburetor needle valve; a prop can lose a blade without warning, possibly costing you an eye. (Gravel and dirt can be picked up by a prop's airflow and cause serious damage.) When another pilot is starting his engine, step to the rear of his plane, and hold his fuselage—grasp it just ahead of the fin and on the side opposite the muffler. He'll think you are a great guy for helping him out (when you are actually staying clear of his propeller for your own safety). If *you* are starting a plane don't trust the other fellow's grip on your fuselage to be perfect; it just might slip and give you a "prop in the leg."

- Use safety glasses at the field. It you wear regular glasses, specify *full safety glass* lenses when you get your next prescription (the same applies to sun glasses); full safety glass costs only a couple of dollars more than standard lenses.

- Use the buddy system. Take a friend to the field with you or go flying when you know someone else will be there. Should you be injured, at least someone will be there to take you to a hospital.

- Always move cautiously around the pit area. If you're not flying or working on your equipment, stay behind the pit area; when you're in the pit area, move only after looking around to see where you are going to put your feet next: a fall at the wrong time can result in personal injury or damage to someone's plane.

Even though there are many groups like the DCRC club, there will never be too many. It is not unusual to find a club's membership filled. Club charters often state a membership limit between 40 and 50; this prevents clubs from getting too large and unmanageable, and also prevents the disappointment that comes with traveling miles to a club site and finding the activity so hectic and air traffic so dense as to make flying a drag. If you can't locate a club nearby, start one: visit your local hobby shop and get the names of RC fliers in your area; band together, hold a meeting, elect officers—and you're on your way.

11

RC Helicopters

A helicopter gets its lift using a *vertical screw*, its upward pointing prop, which turns more slowly than the props on its conventional counterparts: full-sized planes or models. Although a helicopter's main rotor (there are two, one being in the tail) might be thought of as "screwing" the craft up into the atmosphere, like any other prop it has the shape of an airfoil: as the prop turns, air pressure is reduced on the side facing away from the fuselage and lift is created. The rotor mounted horizontally in the tail counteracts the craft's tendency to rotate around the axis of the main rotor when its speed is exactly right, its lift counterbalances the main rotor's torque. Because the body is thus stabilized, the helicopter can be made to maneuver forward, backward, or sideways, much like regular aircraft. (Of course, conventional aircraft cannot move backward like helicopters.)

HOW IT WORKS

The tail rotor (Fig. 11-1) is controlled, to produce its stabilizing effect, in two ways: either its speed or pitch is changed. In models, however, it is easier to keep the tail rotor turning at a constant speed and vary its pitch.

To change a model helicopter's heading (compass direction), the pitch of the tail rotor is changed (just a little) by radio control; when the model turns to the desired

Fig. 11-1. Helicopter tail rotor having variable-pitch blades. The speed of the tail rotor is adjusted by radio control to make the model point toward the desired heading.

direction, the rotor's pitch is brought back to that necessary to hold the new heading. As you might imagine, this control must be adjusted constantly in a wind. For movement along a helicopter's pitch and roll axes (back and forth and side to side), the main prop must be tilted, so it not only creates lift for maintaining altitude, it creates lift to move the craft

Fig. 11-2. The cyclic control paddles are perpendicular to the main rotor. This Kavan Jet Ranger is hard to distinguish from the real thing in flight.

176

forward or backward. This is accomplished by using cyclic control paddles mounted perpendicular to the main prop, as illustrated in Fig. 11-2, for example. The pitch of the control paddles is controlled by a *swash plate* (Fig. 11-3) located below the main prop in the helicopter body. When a *left* control signal is sent to the receiver in a model helicopter, it causes the swash plate to tilt down on the left, making each control paddle change its angle of attack one way on that side, and the other way on the other side; they are neutrally positioned while passing through fore and aft positions of rotation, where they have no influence on the helicopter. The result of this up and down movement during a left or right command causes the model to rotate on its roll axis (counterclockwise as viewed from the back). This in turn changes the direction of the main prop's lift from exactly vertical to a little left of vertical: a sideways force is added to the upward force and the model moves to the left. Its speed is dependent on the roll angle and the speed of the main prop. The swash plate can be tilted toward the front, back, left, and right, each position governed

Fig. 11-3. The swash plate (seen here in a Kavan Jet Ranger) is tilted by radio control to make the control paddles deflect.

by a distinct radio-control signal; a combination signal is used to affect changes to inbetween positions. In some systems the main prop is changed in pitch like the control paddles. In this case, directional control can be accomplished without the control paddles shown. But this arrangement requires more control power of a steering mechanism, the reason the method shown is used most.

FLYING IT

To control a model helicopter using radio, four channels are needed: one for main prop speed to govern up and down movement (corresponding to the throttle control on a model airplane), one for right and left turns (analogous to the rudder channel on a model plane), one for back and forth movement (a model airplane's elevator channel), and one for controlling the tail rotor for rotation around the yaw axis (instead of ailerons).

Flying a model helicopter entails increasing the speed of the main prop until the craft takes off. This is simple enough, but as soon as the model is airborne, the speed of the tail rotor must be adjusted to prevent a spin. Maneuvers in the air are made by sending a command (left or right, forward or backward) or a combination of commands. Moving the control stick for the tail rotor (normally rudder control in airplanes) left makes the nose go to the left. Some pilots *fly the tail*: the tail goes in the same direction the stick is moved. The throttle lever is the same as for other aircraft; the stick is moved up for full throttle, and down for the converse effect. The main rotor is tilted forward by operating it as if it were the elevator of a regular model. Pushing the stick forward (down elevator for an airplane) causes the control paddles to change the main rotor's angle. Tilted forward, the rotor makes the helicopter go forward (Fig. 11-4); an opposite control command makes it go backward. The lateral (side-to-side) paddle control is operated by the aileron stick on the transmitter, which is moved to change the tail's direction, causing the craft to move sideways. All four controls must be used at the same time to keep a helicopter hovering: stationary in the air. The throttle has to be controlled constantly while the tail rotor is made to compensate for main-rotor torque. Generally it is easier for a helicopter to hover when there is a wind.

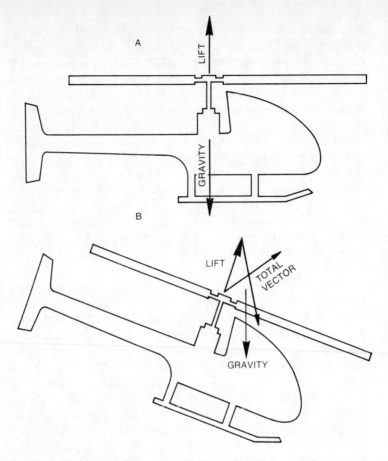

Fig. 11-4. The force vectors at work when a helicopter is made to move forward; in A the helicopter is hovering (the control paddles are neutral); in B the control paddles have been deflected.

Commonly, tail rotor pitch can be adjusted by turning the clevis (fitting) on the pushrod leading to the rotor (rudder) servo to prevent the tail from turning during takeoffs.

Forward movement is obtained by pushing the transmitter stick (normally used for elevator control) forward, thereby making the cyclic paddles change the main rotor blades' angle of attack for forward movement.

Some helicopters have a fifth control, *collective pitch*, that adjusts main rotor pitch (in the blades). Landing is accomplished by simply throttling down the main rotor until the model settles to the ground.

Helicopters require large engines to turn their relatively massive props. They are cooled by a small fan with a shroud to direct its airflow. Starting these engines (using a belt) can be tricky: unless you stay clear of the rotating prop, you could experience pilot blackout at ground level. Setting the model on a platform is one approach to dealing with this hazard; it gets the prop well above the pilot. Another approach is to lie on the ground under the prop. When a rotor blade is arcing forward while the model is moving forward, the relative airflow past the blade is faster than when the blade is arcing rearward. Normally this would give the blade more lift when moving forward than when it is moving back. Ideally, when a helicopter is moving, its rotor blades would adjust automatically for less pitch when arcing toward the direction of the aircraft's motion, and for greater pitch when turning away from it.

A helicopter must be trimmed for flight like any other model aircraft. This entails hanging the helicopter by a cord attached to the center of the rotor shaft (with the rotor head removed). A small level is laid on the transmission plate (at the bottom of the rotor shaft) to level the craft along its pitch axis, and across the back as a check for leveling along the roll axis. Corrections are made by weighing either the nose or the front of the right skid (landing structure). The nose should be down slightly when the fuel tank is full. The tail rotor is adjusted by using the transmitter trim lever while the helicopter is hovering about 5 feet above the ground; if the trim lever requires too much movement, the tail rotor stick is adjusted. When the model is on the ground (and quiescent) the clevis on the servo pushrod can be adjusted so the rotor's speed is about right when the tail rotor trim lever and stick are in neutral.

Before flying an RC helicopter, check that the control paddles and the swash plate are level (neutral). The main rotor should have a little play in it when it is adjusted for the correct angle of attack (usually about 5°). The rotor blades should be balanced precisely to avoid excessive vibration (instructions for this procedure are given with most helicopter kits). After each flight, check all nuts and bolts, and any other parts that might have been affected by vibration, for tightness of fit; the high levels of vibration produced by helicopters can easily shake a part loose. A helicopter's motor should always be started with the controls in the low throttle position; too fast a start can damage the clutch and gears. For the motor to run properly, the fuel/air mixture must be slightly rich. It can be made leaner by adjusting the needle valve as necessary for best performance, as long as you are careful not to stall the motor.

Laying out and installing four-channel RC gear for a model helicopter is not usually a problem; there is room galore. But

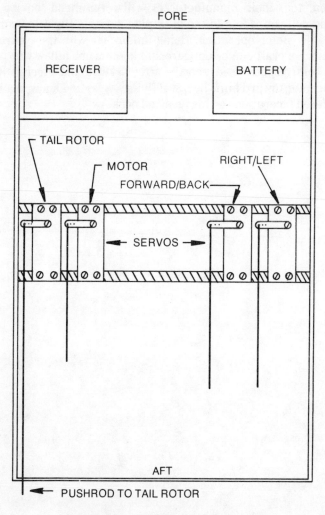

MODEL HELICOPTER RC INSTALLATION

Fig. 11-5. Four-channel RC system layout for a model helicopter.

its placement must take into account flight characteristics peculiar to these craft. You not only have to worry about pitch balance, you must consider roll balance (a model airplane, having wings, doesn't have a tendency to roll). Figure 11-5 depicts a layout typical for a model helicopter.

Some of the problems associated with helicopter flight are overheating leading to engine destruction, breaking starting belts, and electrical interference from scraping rotor parts. Often, too, their manufacturers will recommend leaving a nicad cell connected to the glow plug during a flight to insure reliable motor operation. Being unfamiliar with the controls for such a craft can be dangerous. I know of one fellow who got his controls confused shortly after takeoff and steered his helicopter toward him; he's still flying, as far as I know, but he suffered lacerations on his face and neck.

Appendices

Appendices

Appendix A

NATIONAL DISTRIBUTION OF RC CLUBS

NUMBER OF CLUBS

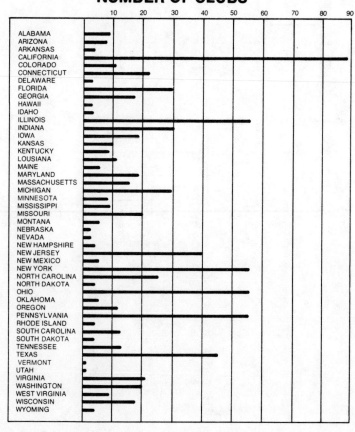

Appendix B

REPRESENTATION OF RC AIRCRAFT TYPES

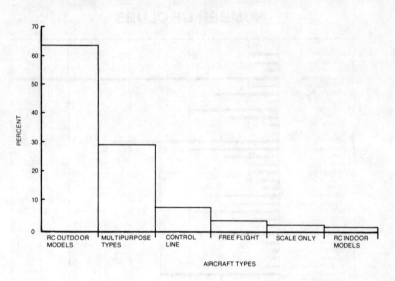

Appendix C

RC FREQUENCIES COLOR CODE

FREQUENCY (MHz)	COLOR(S)
26.995	Brown
27.045	Red
27.095	Orange
27.145	Yellow
27.195	Green
27.255	Blue
53.10	Brown & Black
53.20	Red & Black
53.30	Orange & Black
53.40	Yellow & Black
53.50	Green & Black
72.08	Brown & White
72.16	Light Blue & White
72.24	Red & White
72.32	Violet & White
72.40	Orange & White
72.64	Green & White
72.96	Yellow & White

Index